CAMBRIDGE
UNIVERSITY PRESS

CAMBRIDGE Global English

for Cambridge Primary English as a Second Language

Workbook 6

Jane Boylan & Claire Medwell

Series Editor: Kathryn Harper

CAMBRIDGE
UNIVERSITY PRESS

University Printing House, Cambridge CB2 8BS, United Kingdom

One Liberty Plaza, 20th Floor, New York, NY 10006, USA

477 Williamstown Road, Port Melbourne, VIC 3207, Australia

314–321, 3rd Floor, Plot 3, Splendor Forum, Jasola District Centre, New Delhi – 110025, India

103 Penang Road, #05–06/07, Visioncrest Commercial, Singapore 238467

Cambridge University Press is part of the University of Cambridge.

It furthers the University's mission by disseminating knowledge in the pursuit of education, learning and research at the highest international levels of excellence.

www.cambridge.org
Information on this title: www.cambridge.org/9781108810906

First published 2014
Second edition published 2022

20 19 18 17 16 15 14 13 12 11 10 9 8 7 6 5 4 3 2

Printed in Dubai by Oriental Press

A catalogue record for this publication is available from the British Library

ISBN 978-1-108-81090-6 Workbook with Digital Access (1 Year)

Additional resources for this publication at www.cambridge.org/9781108810906

Contents

How to use this book

This workbook provides questions for you to practise what you have learned in class. There is a unit to match each unit in your Learner's Book.

Tips to help you with your learning. →

> **Writing tip**
>
> **Connecting words**
>
> Use **connecting words** to organise your ideas logically and help readers follow the points in your essay.
>
> **Firstly**, when you have pocket money you ...
>
> ... pocket money is a good idea **because** it teaches us to manage money ourselves.

Information to help you find out more about grammar. →

> **Use of English**
>
> We can use ***will*** to make predictions about the future. For the negative, we can say ***will not*** or ***won't***.
>
> I **will** be a scientist
> We'**ll** all have electric cars.
> Cities **won't** be as polluted.
> **Will** people ride electric bikes more?

Use the Cambridge Learner Corpus to get your grammar right! →

> **Get it right!**
>
> Be careful with irregular plural nouns with the present simple.
>
> People don't ~~lives~~ all year round on the ice in Antarctica.
>
> People don't live all year round on the ice in Antarctica.
>
> Other irregular nouns are: *men*, *women*, *fish* and *species*.

Each Use of English lesson is divided into three parts:

Focus: these grammar questions help you to master the basics. →

> **Focus**
>
> 1 **Find out about the history of the telephone. Complete the text with verbs in the past simple.**
>
> Alexander Graham Bell is known for inventing the telephone in the late 1800s. He [1] ___was___ (be) born in Scotland in 1847 and [2] ________ (become) interested in the science of sound because both his mother and wife [3] ________ (be) deaf. He loved doing experiments and eventually he was able to send voice signals down a telephone wire.
>
> The first telephone call [4] ________ (take) place in March 1876 between Alexander Graham Bell and his assistant Thomas Watson. The telephone he [5] ________ (use) was tall and long and you [6] ________ (have) to use a separate mouth and ear piece, one to listen and one to speak. As design developed people [7] ________ (begin) to use a round dial with numbers. Now we use wireless phones, which let us talk and move around the house at the same time.

Practice: these grammar questions help you to become more accurate and confident. →

Practice

2 Kofi has saved his pocket money and wants to buy a new football shirt. Circle and number the six errors in the conversation, then write the corrections at the end.

Kofi: There's the City shirt and the National kit. I don't know which one to buy!

Dad: Well, which one will you wear the oftenest do you think? 1

Kofi: The City shirt, because we go to City games all the time ... but I like the National shirt more better!

Dad: OK, but I think that shirt costs much than the other one. Have you checked?

Kofi: Oh yes, it's more expensive. I think I've got enough pocket money ...

Dad: OK then, try them both on. Let's see which one fits better.

Kofi: The National shirt definitely fits the best but it costs the more! I don't know what to do!

Dad: Mmm ... and the City shirt is a bit too big – it fits looser, but that is a good thing because you are growing more faster this year than ever before!

Kofi: So the City shirt will last the most longest?

Challenge: these questions will help you use language fluently and prepare for the next level. →

Challenge

5 Complete the job advert with your own ideas.

- We are looking for a (adjective) and (adjective) (job title)
- Experience need – (why?) ___________
- Must be good at ... (?) ___________
- Must be knowledgeable about ... (?) ___________
- Must be interested in ... (?) ___________
- Interviews will be held in the ... (where?) ___________

Questions that cover what you have learned in the unit. If you can answer these, you are ready to move on to the next unit. →

› 2.6 Check your progress

1 Look at the list of places and equipment. Write the name of the sport.

a stick, hard ball, shin pads ___________

b trunks, goggles, towel ___________

c racket, net, shuttlecock ___________

d net, ball, beach ___________

e trainers, track, tracksuit ___________

Questions to help you think about how you learn. →

› 4.7 Reflection

Think about what you have studied in this unit. Answer the questions.

1 What topics did you like and why?

____

2 What activities did you like and why?

____

3 What did you find challenging and why?

____

1 My world

1.1 What connects us to others?

1 **Vocabulary: Emotions**

Find and circle the six emotions that start with these letters in the word search. Use the pictures to help you.

a

h________

b

n________

c

i________

H	U	V	J	C	E	T	S	L	V	Y	E
M	M	Q	K	P	Y	X	H	Y	R	B	U
J	D	I	K	O	N	P	K	G	M	H	W
T	M	U	N	R	Z	P	N	C	E	Z	H
K	Q	L	A	T	(H	A	P	P	Y)	E	H
T	J	Y	J	S	E	V	Q	L	I	T	D
U	N	F	X	N	E	R	V	O	U	S	N
V	R	U	K	P	J	I	E	M	E	V	L
B	K	P	P	C	H	H	M	S	F	V	D
E	X	C	I	T	E	D	J	L	T	M	H
K	W	P	M	S	C	A	R	E	D	E	C
N	J	J	O	U	Q	G	G	P	Y	V	D

d

s________

e

a________

f

e________

2 **How do the different experiences in Activity 1 make the children feel? Complete these sentences with your opinion.**

a Ice cream makes her feel happy because ______________________.

b He feels __________ because ______________________.

c He's really __________ in ______________________.

d She's really __________ because ______________________.

e He gets __________ when ______________________.

f We are __________ when we ______________________.

3 **Complete these sentences with a positive or negative word.**

cool	win	pollution	scratch	starve	awesome

a You can design and build some really __________ buildings on that video game!

b It makes me angry when there is no fresh air because of __________ from cars and factories.

c My new pet kitten likes to __________ all the furniture.

d When people cut down the rainforests, animals lose their habitat and they __________.

e I love playing board games, especially when I __________!

f That is the most __________ sports car I've ever seen!

Challenge

4 **Draw three pictures which you connect with each of these emotions. Write reasons why in your notebook.**

a Happy

b Angry

c Excited

1.2 Present perfect

Use of English

We can use the **present perfect** to talk about indefinite time in the past.

My dad **has visited** many countries, but he **hasn't been** to China.

today

(dad has visited many countries up to now)

past

We often use adverbs with the present perfect too. We use **yet** to mean any time up to now.

Have you **finished** your lunch **yet**?

We use **ever** in questions to talk about an experience up to the present.

Have you **ever had** a scary experience?

We use ***just*** to talk about the recent past.

Yes, I'**ve just seen** a spider in the cupboard.

Focus

1 **What has Amara done so far today? Use the notes to help you. Write sentences in the present perfect.**

a visit / grandparents She's visited her grandparents.

b have / lunch with family ______

c be / on / a bike ride with her friends ______

d watch / some videos online ______

e make / pizza with her sister ______

f read / a chapter / of her new book ______

Get it right!

Remember to use the correct auxiliary verb.

~~I'm~~ *I've put my desk near the window.*

Practice

2 **Aliya is preparing for a big swimming competition. Complete the dialogue. Use the correct form of the verb or choose an adverb from the box.**

~~pack~~	be	yet	put	have	just	take part

Mum: [1] Have you packed your swimming bag [2] ____________?

Aliya: Yes, and I've [3] ____________ had a text message from Saul – he's waiting for me outside. He's [4] ____________ there for five minutes.

Mum: OK. Well good luck. I'm sure you'll win.

Aliya: I'm not sure. I'm really nervous and I've never [5] ____________ in such a big swimming competition before.

Mum: Relax – you'll be awesome! Oh, and I haven't [6] ____________ a snack in your bag, so here's some money.

Aliya: Thanks Mum. See you later.

Challenge

3 **Write a dialogue about an experience or an event between yourself and a friend. Use the present perfect and the adverbs *ever*, *yet* and *just*. Think of your own idea or continue the dialogue below.**

Amara: Have you ever been to a pop concert?

Maya: No, I haven't.

____

____

____

1.3 Prepositions before nouns

Use of English

Prepositions give us more information about the nouns in a sentence, for example where something or someone is. Common prepositions are *on*, *in*, *at*, *from*.

1 Location

At: specific locations, addresses, shops, events

I'm **at** Wei's house. Ellie isn't **at** the party.

On: single mountains, planets, beaches, islands, public transport

I'm **on** the bus.
I'm **on** a desert island.

In: buildings, cities, countries, continents, groups of people

I couldn't see Anna **in** the crowd.
Do you live **in** Italy?

2 Origin

I'm **from** Indonesia.
Latitude lines circle the Earth **from** east to west.

Focus

1 **Read about Eva's incredible holiday.**
Circle the correct preposition in each sentence.

a I had an amazing holiday **in / on** Asia.
b We flew **to / from** London, Heathrow, to Bangkok.
c **On / From** the airport terminal, we got **in / on** the bus to the city centre.
d We stayed **at / on** Paradise Point hotel on a main street in the city.
e We visited all the sights **from / in** the city.
f One day, I got lost **on / in** a crowd of people, but my dad quickly found me!

Get it right!

from + origin

The famous architect ~~in~~ **from** China was interviewed on TV.

Practice

2 **Read about the most southern capital city in the world. Complete the text with the correct prepositions.**

Wellington [1] ___in___ New Zealand is the most southern capital [2] ________ the world and also the windiest!

This remote place takes a long time for many people to get to. If you get [3] ________ a plane [4] ________ the UK, it would take about 24 hours to get there. Imagine flying [5] ________ the sky for that long!

The city has a population of 415,000 people, not many for a capital city, but only five million people live [6] ________ the entire country! People [7] ________ New Zealand have a popular 'nickname'. They are called 'Kiwis' after the exotic bird that lives [8] ________ the islands.

Challenge

3 **Write about Reykjavik, the most northern capital city in the world. Investigate online to find out about its location, population, inhabitants and other interesting facts.**

____
____
____
____
____
____

1.4 A first time for everything

1 **Read and match the descriptions of first-time experiences to a picture.**

a 

b 

c 

1

I've only been rock climbing once in my life. I tried it last year for the first time (in a sports centre, not outside on real rocks!). I've always been afraid of heights but my friend persuaded me to have a go. It was amazing! Afterwards my friend told me I was very brave! *Callum, age 12*

2

I've seen lots of elephants and in my country it's quite normal to see them. But the first time I saw one, I was terrified! Now I think elephants are beautiful, majestic animals. *Sumalee, age 12*

3

I was so excited when I learned to ride a bike! I was very proud of myself because I was only four years old. My dad helped me to learn and he looked at me with satisfaction as I cycled off up the road! *Jaya, age 13*

2 **Find words and short phrases in each description that express:**

- what each child did
- why it was special
- how it felt

Callum: ______________________________

Sumalee: ______________________________

Jaya: ______________________________

3 **Complete these sentences with an adjective or a noun from Activity 1. Use a different word in each sentence.**

a I have a fear of flying, so the first time I flew in a plane I was ___________.

b The woman who rescued the child was so ___________.

c I've failed the maths exam twice, so I feel very ___________ of myself because today I passed it.

d I couldn't sit still because I was so ___________ about winning the prize.

e I looked at my finished painting with ___________.

4 **Look at the underlined parts of the descriptions in Activity 1. Which verb patterns do they match?**

a verb + object

b verb + object + infinitive (with **to**)

5 **Write a description about a first-time experience you have had.**

- Use interesting nouns and adjectives to describe your feelings.
- Write sentences in the past simple and present perfect to describe it.
- Draw a picture about your experience.

1.5 A Girl Called Owl

1 **Read the story in the Learner's Book again.**
Answer these questions with information from the text.

a How is the girl similar to an owl?

____

____

b What does 'Owl' think about owls?

____

c What do Owl's friends think about her mum?

____

d What would you see if you walked into Owl's bedroom?

____

e Why do you think Owl's friend Mallory bought her a birthday card with a puffin on it?

____

2 **Complete this description about an owl using words from the story.**

An owl has [1]f<u>eathers</u>______ and a [2]b____________.
It can [3]f____________.
It [4]h____________ at night.
Its [5]h____________ rotates 360 degrees.

3 **This is a portrait of Owl's mum.**
In your own notebook, describe her using the words provided.

4 **Complete the sentences using words from the box.**

feathers	~~swooped~~	intense	whirly	masses	inherited

a The eagle swooped down to hunt its prey.

b ________ cover a bird's body.

c She ________ her curly, red hair from her mother.

d The pain in her knee was so ________ that she decided to see the doctor.

e Alice drew a ________ pattern on the paper with lots of different colours.

f She has ________ of short, curly, blond hair.

5 **Answer these questions.**

a Why do you think Owl thinks her name is stupid?

____

b Owl's friends 'love' her mum. Why do you think this annoys her?

____

c Do you know why you were given your name(s)? Do you like it/them?

____

d If you could choose any name, what would it be?

____

6 Values: **Accepting our differences**

How do you think you are different from other people?
For example, My friend likes reading and I like music.
She tells me about books and I play her music.

____

____

____

1.6 Check your progress

Choose the correct answers and write in the space.

1 He gets very ________ when he has an exam.
a excited b happy c nervous

2 This video game has really ________ characters who go on incredible adventures.
a awesome b win c interested

3 The ________ in the oceans is killing marine life.
a air b pollution c habitat

4 Mosquito bites make me ________ my skin.
a starve b scratch c cool

5 Have you seen that film ________? It's brilliant!
a just b ever c yet

6 I've ________ started my lunch. Can you call me later?
a yet b just c ever

7 We've been ________ a school trip to an animal sanctuary today.
a in b on c at

8 My mum told me ________ my bedroom.
a clean b organising c to tidy up

9 How long does it take a plane to fly ________ Shanghai to New York?
a in b from c on

10 He showed incredible ________ when he rescued the child from the house on fire.
a bravery b brave c proud

11 I ________ my big, brown eyes from my Spanish father.
a swooped b inherited c harm

12 A bird uses its ________ for eating and feeding its babies.
a beak b feathers c wings

1.7 Reflection

Think about what you have studied in this unit. Answer the questions.

1 What topics did you like and why?

____

____

2 What activities did you like and why?

____

____

3 What did you find challenging and why?

____

____

4 What help do you need now?

____

____

5 What do you want to find out more about?

____

____

2 Sport

2.1 What can we get from sport?

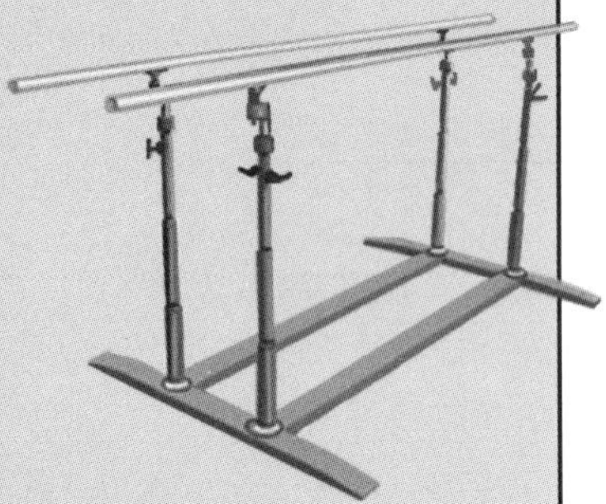

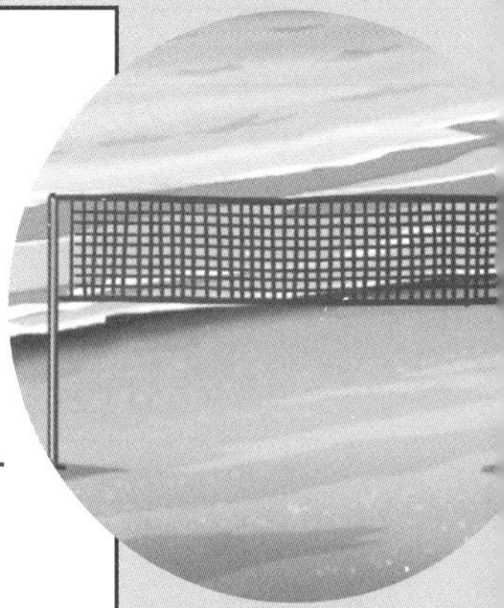

1 Vocabulary: Sports

Do the *Name the Sport* quiz. Read the definitions and write the names of the sports. Use the pictures to help you.

a You do this sport in water. ____________

b You play this sport in a team. You need a circular net and a ball. ____________

c You need to be very flexible and strong to do this sport. ____________

d You hit a ball over a net with a racquet. Two or four people can play this game. ____________

e You need a stick and a hard ball to play this game in teams. ____________

f Sports on a track or field such as running or jumping and throwing competitions. ____________

g This is often played in teams on the beach. You hit a ball over a high net. ____________

h This is a popular team game. You run and kick a ball into a net. ____________

i Two people fight with their arms, hands, legs and feet and try to throw each other over. ____________

j You play this on grass or on a court. You need a net, racquet and shuttlecocks. ____________

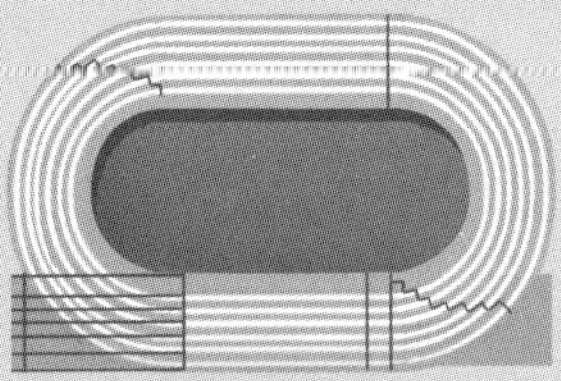

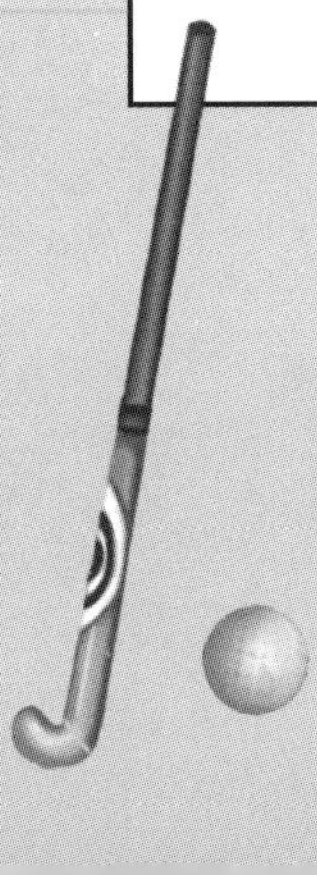

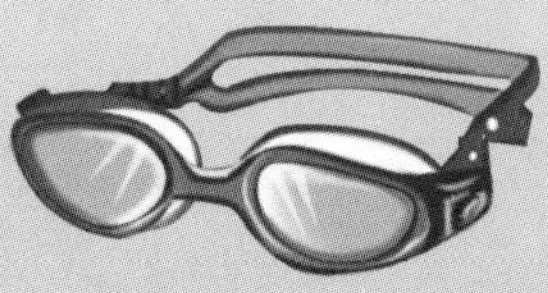

2 **Read about Nadine and Dani's favourite sports. Complete the table with words from the descriptions.**

a I love playing volleyball because it's easy to learn and great fun! All you need is a volleyball and a net. It's played by two six-player teams on a court or on the beach. The object is to hit the ball over the net with your hands. The other team have to try to hit it back before it touches the ground. If not, your team wins a point.

Nadine

b I started playing this game two years ago after going to see a tennis championship. It was so exciting to watch, I knew I had to try it! It's played on a grass or clay court. You can play singles with two players or doubles with four players. You hit a ball with a racquet over a net to your opponent who hits it back. If they miss the ball or it hits the net, your opponent wins a point.

Dani

	Sport	Where do you play it?	How many people play?	Equipment
a	Volleyball			
b				

Challenge

3 **Write about a sport you practise or watch. Use words and verbs from Activity 2 to describe it. Write about:**

a Location ____________________

b People ____________________

c Equipment ____________________

d An opinion ____________________

2.2 First conditional with *if / unless*

Use of English

We use the **first conditional** to talk about situations in the future which we think are possible.

The *if* clause tells you **the condition.** The main clause tells you **the result.**

If you exercise, you'll feel good.

We can use the main clause first but this doesn't change the meaning. We always use a comma if the ***if*** clause is first.

***If** you practise every day, you'll win.*
You'll win if you practise every day.

We can use *unless* instead of *if*. It's the same as *if not*.

***Unless** you practise every day, you won't win.*

Focus

1 **Rita has got a big gymnastics competition next month. Read and circle the correct word in each sentence.**

a If she **trains / will train** hard, she**'ll do / does** well in the competition.

b Unless she **eats / will eat** well, she **will / won't** have any energy.

c She **will be / is** in tip-top condition, if she **will train / trains** hard.

d If she **believes / will believe** in herself, she **will do / won't do** well.

e Unless she **sleeps / will sleep** well before the competition, she **will / won't** perform well.

f If she **feels / will feel** nervous before the competition, she**'ll need / needs** to breathe deeply.

Practice

2 **Read Han's list of study tips. Write full sentences in the first conditional with *if* or *unless*.**

Get it right!

Remember don't use *will* in the *if* clause.

If you ~~will~~ join the sports club, you'**ll** make new friends. ✗

If you join the sports club, you'**ll** make new friends. ✓

a Relax / study well ______

b Go to bed early / feel fresh ______

c Remember better / use pictures ______

d Quiet place to study / concentrate well ______

e Make good notes / remember information better ______

______

Challenge

3 **Write your own tips about good study habits. Make sentences using *unless* or *if*.**

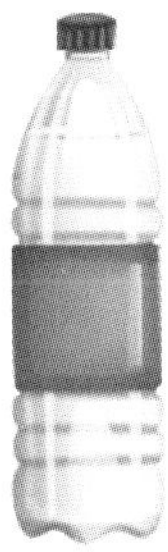

If you sleep well, you'll study better.

______

______

______

______

2.3 need / should / mustn't for advice

Use of English

We use *need* + infinitive with to, to express something that is necessary.

You **need to** train hard to win the race.

We use *should* to give advice.
We use *should* + infinitive without to.

You **should** stretch your muscles after exercise.

We use *must* + infinitive without to, to give strong advice against something.

You **mustn't** eat just before you do exercise.

Focus

1 **Read Omer's running tips.**
Circle the correct word in each sentence.

a You **need / mustn't** run without warming up first.

b When you warm up, you **need / should** stretch your muscles too.

c You **should / mustn't** force your muscles when you stretch or you might hurt yourself.

d You **need / must** to have good trainers or you'll get injured.

e You **mustn't / don't need** to drink water while you are running, but you **should / mustn't** drink water before.

f You **mustn't / should** run too fast to begin with or you won't finish the race.

Practice

2 **Read about where yoga comes from. Circle and number the five errors in the text. Write the corrections at the end.**

> **Get it right!**
>
> Remember to use the correct spelling.
>
> ~~musn't~~ mustn't ~~shoud~~ should

Where does yoga come from?

Yoga is a type of exercise that originated in India and is thousands of years old. You shoud try yoga if you want a strong, flexible body and a relaxed mind. There are millions of people from all over the world who agree! But first there are some facts you need know.
Yoga is great for kids of all ages, but you musn't try difficult yoga without an instructor because you might hurt yourself. You shouldn't to do yoga without warming up first. And you need wear comfortable clothing. When you do the poses, you mustn't to take in deep, long breaths in and out; if you do this, you will feel more energetic and relaxed at the same time. If you want to try a yoga exercise, try the warrior pose in the picture!

a should_______ c __________ e __________

b __________ d __________

Challenge

3 **Imagine you are giving training advice to the children in the pictures. Write sentences using *should/need to* or *mustn't*.**

a ____

b ____

c ____

2.4 Our favourite sports stars

1 **Have you ever played basketball?**
Do you know the names of any famous basketball players?

2 **Read the biography of Lebron James.**
Match the headings 1–4 to the paragraphs A–D.

1 His journey to stardom
2 Present-day success
3 Information about his childhood
4 Amazing facts!

A Lebron James is one of the best players in basketball today. In 2018 he signed a four-year deal with the Los Angeles Lakers for $154 million. He is known for his amazing leaping ability, height and **strength.**

B He was born in Akron, Ohio, USA, on 30 December 1984. His family life was difficult because his father disappeared when he was young and his family didn't have much money. He studied at St Vincent–St Mary High School in Ohio and helped his team win three state titles. He earned the name 'Mr Basketball' for his incredible **talent.**

C After leaving college early, Lebron joined the NBA's Cleveland Cavaliers and became a star overnight! He helped the Miami Heat to win titles in 2012 and 2013, and when he moved back to Cleveland he led the team to its first championship title in 2016 before joining the Lakers in 2018.

D Lebron is over two metres tall and was the youngest ever player to be **selected** by the NBA at the age of 18. Curiously, he's left-handed, but usually shoots with his right hand. His latest **nickname** is King James because many believe he is the best basketball player for over a **decade**!

3 **Match the words in bold from the biography to their definitions.**

a When you are strong, you have a lot of this. ____________

b When you have a special ability for something you have this. ____________

c A period of ten years. ____________

d When you are chosen for a team. ____________

e A familiar or funny name given to a person. ____________

4 **Why are these dates and numbers important in Lebron's story?**

a $154 million ____________

b 2018 ____________

c 1984 ____________

d two metres ____________

e 18 ____________

5 **Use the information in the fact file to write about rising sports star Khadijah Mellah.**

Fact File

Born: 2000 **Country:** South London, UK

Sport: horse-racing

Journey to success: Loves horses / mum sees leaflet for Ebony Horse Club in Brixton / starts horse-riding in 2013

Present day success: August 2019 wins Magnolia Cup at Goodwood racecourse.

Amazing fact: first British Muslim woman to win a horserace at Goodwood

Khadijah was born in South London.

____

____

____

____

2.5 Off Side

1 **Read the extract again from *Off Side* by Tom Palmer. Decide if the sentences are true or false. Correct the false sentences.**

a Danny and his dad go to every game their football team plays at home. True

b Danny's dad is deaf. ______________

c In the story, Danny and his dad are watching a match between the teams, City and United. ______________

d During the match, Danny describes what's happening to his dad. ______________

e The star City players, Anthony Owusu and Sam Roberts, are defenders. ______________

f During the match, Sam Roberts scores a goal. ______________

g When the goal happens, the United fans cheer very loudly. ______________

h After the goal, Danny explains to his dad what has happened. ______________

2 **Think about the story and answer the questions.**

a Did you like the story? What did / didn't you like about it?

____

____

b Did you understand the story better by listening to it, as well as reading it? How does listening make a difference?

____

____

3 **Find the words in blue in the story on pages 37 and 38 of the Learner's Book and match them to a definition.**

a extremely good ____________

b to move up and away when (a ball) hits the ground or goal post ____________

c to find something difficult, but to make a great effort ____________

d to react with a strong expression of emotion ____________

e to shoot the ball into the net as fast as a gunshot ____________

f to shoot a ball into the net like a rocket being launched into space ____________

4 **Match the football team roles to a description.**

(goal) keeper | midfield | strikers | defenders

a The main role of these players is to score goals. ____________

b Players in the goal area who try to stop the other team from scoring. ____________

c A player who defends the goal in the area between the goal posts. ____________

d The group of players that connect the defenders and strikers. ____________

5 Values: **Write about any school 'team' that you belong to (for example, a sports team, a project team, being part of a class).**

- Describe the types of duties that you and the other team or class members have.
- How do you feel if it works well? What do you try to do if it doesn't work well?

____

____

____

____

____

2.6 Check your progress

1 **Look at the list of places and equipment. Write the name of the sport.**

- a stick, hard ball, shin pads ____________
- b trunks, goggles, towel ____________
- c racket, net, shuttlecock ____________
- d net, ball, beach ____________
- e trainers, track, tracksuit ____________

2 **Read and match the sentence halves.**

1	If you eat too much chocolate, ...	a	warm up before exercise
2	You should ...	b	to rest if you have an injury.
3	You mustn't ...	c	you'll feel sick.
4	You need...	d	eat a lot of food before doing exercise.
5	Unless you relax...	e	if you don't eat your breakfast.
6	You'll be hungry...	f	you won't do well in the exam.

Challenge

3 **Choose a famous sports star. Imagine you are that person.
Write a 'To do' list about your food, health and training. Use *need*, *should* and *mustn't*.**

To do ...

I need to train hard this week.

____

____

____

____

2.7 Reflection

Think about what you have studied in this unit. Answer the questions.

1 What topics did you like and why?

____

____

2 What activities did you like and why?

____

____

3 What did you find challenging and why?

____

____

4 What help do you need now?

____

____

5 What do you want to find out more about?

____

____

3 Living things

3.1 Strategies for survival

1 **What can you remember about Emperor penguins? Complete the sentences with the correct word.**

chick	breed	mate	hatches	huddle	colony

a Emperor penguins ____________ in March and April each year.

b A group of penguins is called a ____________.

c A baby penguin is called a ____________.

d They ____________ together to protect themselves from the cold.

e A chick ____________ from an egg.

f A penguin's partner is called its ____________.

2 **Complete this article about Emperor penguins for 'Kids of the Earth' magazine. Use your knowledge and circle the correct word.**

Kids of the Earth – Emperor penguins

This month's article is about Emperor penguins. They live in the [1] **Arctic / Antarctic** where temperatures can drop to [2] **−60** °C **/ −40** °C during the winter. The struggle to raise their [3] **chicks / children** is quite dangerous. In the Autumn, males and [4] **women / females** meet to [5] **hunt / mate** and then they wait weeks for the eggs to develop. They protect the egg huddled in their [6] **families / colonies** until it [7] **survives / hatches** in the Spring.

3 'A penguin is born!' Match the sentences below to the pictures they describe.

1 Two months later the chick hatches. ________

2 The female meets a mate to breed. ___a___

3 The males protect the eggs huddled together in the colony. ________

4 The female penguin needs to feed in the ocean. ________

5 The female penguin passes the egg to its mate with her feet. ________

6 The female lays the egg and protects it with her lower body. ________

a 

b 

c 

d 

e 

f 

Challenge

4 Investigate online to find out about another Antarctic animal. Write some sentences about your findings. Include information about its characteristics and diet.

____

____

____

____

____

____

3.2 Present simple

Use of English

Another use of the **present simple** is to talk about things which are always true, such as lifecycles of animals or factual information about nature or places.

The Antarctic **is** the fifth biggest continent.
It **has** the largest single mass of ice on Earth.
Not many species **live** in the Antarctic.

We can also use the **present continuous** to talk about changing situations which are happening now.

The ice **is melting**.
Penguins **are suffering** from the effects of climate change.

Focus

1 **How much do you know about Antarctica?**

- Complete the sentences with a verb from the box.
- There are two untrue statements. Can you spot them?

live be come not rain ~~cover~~ not live

a The ice in the Antarctic covers an area of almost 14 million square km.

b The ice ____________ five kilometres deep and it's the largest single mass of ice on Earth.

c It ____________ very often and so it is in fact a desert!

d Lots of different species ____________ there.

e Polar bears ____________ in the Antarctic.

f The name 'Antarctica' ____________ from an Italian word meaning the 'opposite of north.'

Untrue statements: ____

Get it right!

Be careful with irregular plural nouns with the present simple.

People don't ~~lives~~ all year round on the ice in Antarctica.

People don't live all year round on the ice in Antarctica.

Other irregular nouns are: *men*, *women*, *fish* and *species*.

Practice

2 **Read Juan's description about the Antarctic Blue Whale.**
Circle and number the six errors in the text, then write the corrections at the end.

The Antarctic is an extremely cold place so there aren't many species which (lives) there. Penguins, seals, fish and large whales is its main inhabitants.

The Antarctic Blue Whale is the largest animal on the planet. It weighs about 200 tons, that's the weight of 33 elephants and it have a heart the size of a small car!

The Antarctic whale are an endangered species because people hunted whales until 1972. In 2018, there wasn't many, only about 3000 individuals, but in 2020 an expedition counted 55 on just one trip. Scientists feels really positive about seeing whales feeding in the Antarctic again.

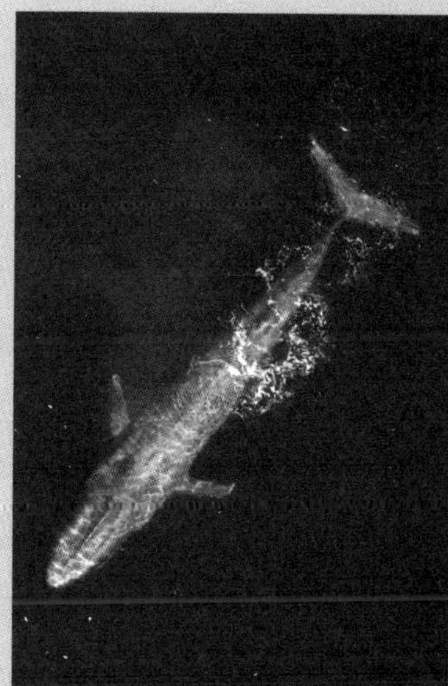

a live
b ______
c ______
d ______
e ______
f ______

Challenge

3 **Find out about another Antarctic animal online.**
Write five quiz questions to ask another classmate.
Write questions about its:

- Characteristics
- Food and diet
- Breeding season

3.3 Relative clauses

Use of English

Defining **relative clauses** give us essential information about something or someone, and tell us which noun we are talking about.

who / that

We can use *who* or *that* to talk about people.

Have you met the girl **who** lives next door?
He's the boy **that** helped me yesterday.

which / that

We can use *which* or *that* to talk about things.

This is the sea animal **which / that** we read about yesterday.

Other relative pronouns

Where can refer to a place.

That's the museum **where** they've got a blue whale.

Whose refers to the person that something belongs to.

This is the book **whose** author is visiting today.

Focus

1 **What do you know about food chains?**
Match the sentence halves to make true sentences.

1 Rabbits are primary consumers ... (matched to b)
2 Plants get energy from the sun ...
3 The countryside is where ...
4 Carnivores are animals ...
5 Omnivores are animals ...
6 Animals ...

a which have no predators are tertiary consumers.
b that only eat plants.
c which eat plants and meat.
d which they use to make food.
e many primary consumers like rabbits and mice live.
f whose main diet is meat.

Get it right!

Don't forget the relative pronoun.

~~I saw something looked like a frog on the road.~~

I saw something **which** looked like a frog on the road.

~~I have some friends are animals lovers just like me.~~

I have some friends **who** are animal lovers just like me.

Practice

2 **Find out about the Ocean Food Chain. Complete the text with relative pronouns.**

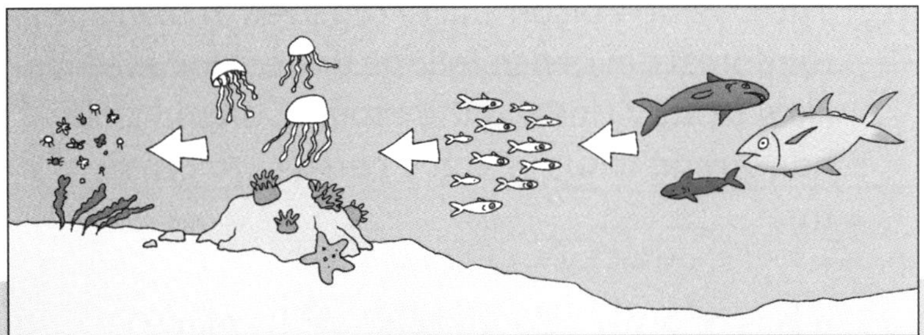

The Ocean Food Chain

Do you know what eats what in the ocean? Well, as with any food chain, the Marine Food Chain begins with plants [1]__________ produce their own food using energy from the sun. A common sea plant is plankton [2]__________ provides vitamins, proteins and minerals for primary consumers to feed on in the next link. This group is made up of small fish [3]__________ float in the sea. Jellyfish and starfish are examples of these. Secondary consumers are common fish like minnows [4]__________ eat the floating ones. Finally, there are the tertiary consumers [5]__________ huge appetite means they eat all the smaller fish. They are usually large fish such as tuna or small sharks. It's a fish-eat-fish world!

Challenge

3 **Investigate and find out information about another food chain in one of these habitats. Draw a diagram to illustrate it and write sentences about it in your notebook.**

desert	mountain	forest	savannah

3.4 Animal types

1 **Why do you think this frog is called the *Dyeing* Poison Dart Frog?**

I think ______________________________

2 **Read the infographic text. Match the pictures to the text.**

1 The Dyeing Poison Dart Frog lives in tropical rainforests in dense foliage under leaves. It likes to stay close to the ground, although it has strong limbs which it can use to climb trees. __b__

2 It has brightly coloured skin with yellow on its back and blue on its legs. It is one of the largest species of poisonous frogs. ______

3 Curiously, unlike most frogs that are nocturnal, poison dart frogs are more sociable during the day. ______

4 It has just one natural predator, a snake which is immune to its poison. ______

5 It is extremely toxic. Indigenous groups in the Amazon used its poison on the tips of their darts and arrows for hunting animals and defending themselves. That's how it got its name! ______

a 

b 

c 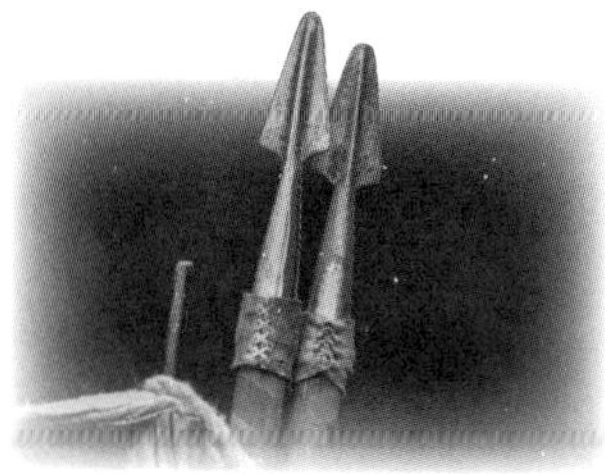

d 

e 

3 **Which part of the text gives information about the frog's:**

a behaviour? ______

b habitat? ______

c characteristics? ______

d origins of its name? ______

e predators? ______

4 **Read the text again. Find an example of:**

a The present simple ______________________

b A defining relative clause ______________________

c A short sentence ______________________

5 **Write an infographic text about a chameleon in your notebook. Use the photos and notes to help you. Write about its habitat, characteristics, diet and behaviour.**

Habitat: mainly rainforests, deserts (Africa)

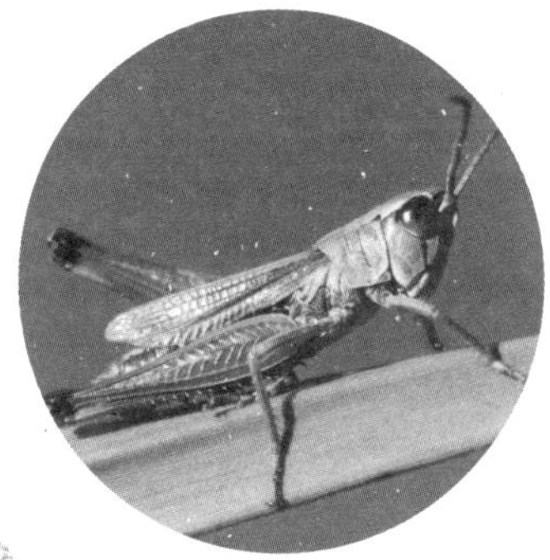

Diet: grasshoppers and stick insects

Chameleon

Characteristics: big eyes, 360-degree view, crested head

Behaviour: Uses tongue to catch prey

3.5 Song for a Whale

1 **Read the extract in the Learner's Book again. Complete these captions describing each picture.**

a This is a whale called Blue 55.

b He swam ______

c He doesn't eat ______

d His mother was ______

e Researchers couldn't ______

2 **Complete the fact file about Blue 55.**

Fact File

Name:

Characteristics:

Diet:

Behaviour:

Curious fact:

3 **Complete this summary about the video in the story using words from the extract.**

hybrid	plankton	marine biologists	~~pod~~
species	sanctuary	migration	ocean

According to the video, Blue 55 is unlike other whales. Firstly, he didn't swim in a [1] pod like other whales. Secondly, he didn't eat squid or seals, instead he ate [2]__________. Blue 55 was a [3]__________, which means his parents had been different [4]__________. [5]__________ working in a [6]__________ also discovered that the sounds he made weren't the same as other whales and his [7]__________ patterns were different too, which explains why he is alone in the [8]__________.

4 **How does the video make Iris feel? Find language that describes this.**

____

5 **How does the writer refer to Blue 55 in the story when she doesn't use his name? Find and write three examples here.**

____

Challenge

6 Values: **Feeling empathy**

a Why do you think Iris felt empathy towards the whale? Write your reason.

I think Iris feels empathy towards Blue 55 because ____________________

____

b **Write a sentence about when you have felt empathy towards a classmate, for example if he/she is upset, feeling unwell, or hurts herself/himself in the playground.**

____

c **Explain how you helped in one of these situations.**

____

3.6 Check your progress

1 **Complete the crossword.**

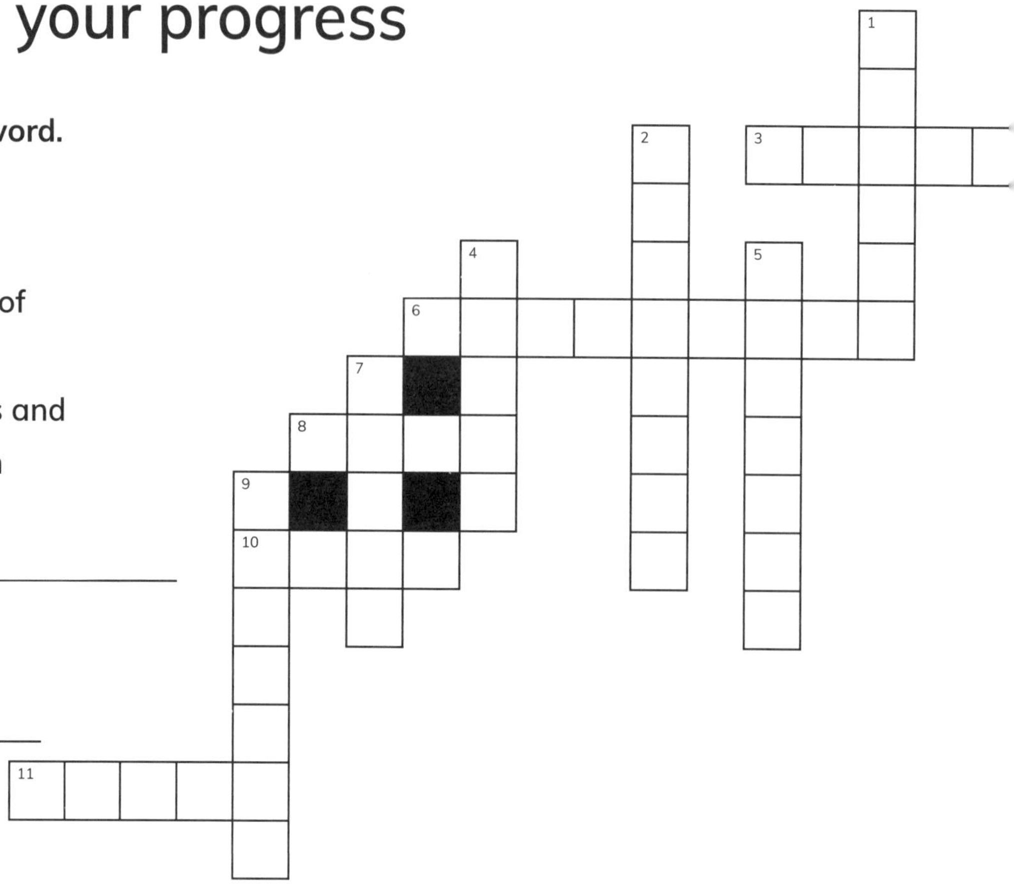

Down ↓

1 What is a group of penguins called?

2 Birds have wings and __________ on their bodies.

4 Penguins eggs __________ in the Spring.

5 A carnivorous plant __________ its prey with the sticky liquid on its leaves.

7 Omnivores eat food __________ comes from meat and plants.

9 There are many different __________ of whale.

Across →

3 A fish has __________ and lungs to breathe.

6 A __________ is a safe place for animals.

8 What do you call a baby penguin?

10 A group of wolves is called a __________.

11 Grasshoppers are herbivores __________ main diet is plants.

Challenge

2 **Make a revision crossword to test your friends!**

3.7 Reflection

Think about what you have studied in this unit. Answer the questions.

1 What topics did you like and why?

2 What activities did you like and why?

3 What did you find challenging and why?

4 What help do you need now?

5 What do you want to find out more about?

4 Inventions

4.1 Gadgets and us

1 **Complete the words and label the gadgets and equipment in the picture.**

a t __ b __ __ t

b __ o __ p a __ s

c s __ a r __ p h __ n __

d m __ u __ t a __ n bike

e h o __ __ r b o __ r __

2 **Complete the descriptions with the children's favourite things from Activity 1.**

a "I can't live without my 1 ______________________. I can research stuff online, message my friends and watch films. The screen is bigger than a phone's so I can see things better too. The only thing I can't do is call my friends and it's a bit too big to carry around in my pocket!"

b "It's got to be my 2 ______________________. I've just got a new one and it's awesome! It's got huge tyres so I can race across grass and tracks. I can't ride it on the sand though; I'd need to buy special tyres to do that."

c "I got my first 3 ______________________ for my birthday this year. It's so cool! Now I can call and message my friends. I can watch videos and play games on it, too. It's also got a brilliant, mega-pixel camera so I'll be taking lots of selfies and photos."

3 **Read Class 6A's summary about their mobile phones and laptops. Then complete and label the pie chart.**

For many of us (40%), the most important reason for using mobile phones and laptops is for entertainment: to download apps and play games. But for 35%, the most important reason is to communicate with each other through calling, messaging and sometimes Facetime and Skype.

Then, for 15% of us, the reasons are more practical, such as to store information. That includes saving files for schoolwork, saving useful websites as favourites, and also for storing photos and videos.

Finally, for 10% of us, the most important reason is to be creative – so that includes taking and editing photos as well as making videos.

Class 6A's reasons for using mobile phones and laptops

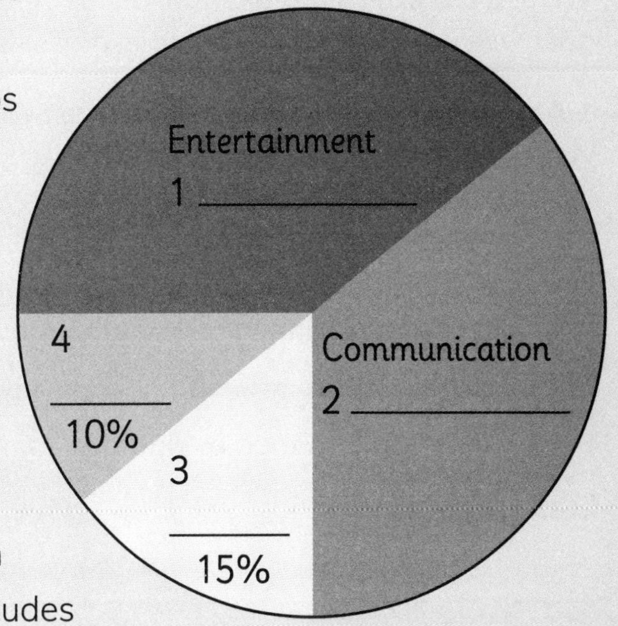

Challenge

4 **Complete the sentences about the gadgets and equipment that you and your family use.**

a My favourite gadget has got to be ____________.

b I can use it to ____________.

c Another gadget that I use a lot is ____________.

d The most important gadget in my family is ____________.

e We think it's ____________ than ____________ because ____________.

4.2 Past simple review

Use of English

We use the **past simple** to talk about definite time in the past. We can use different time expressions.

1 A definite point in time: in 2020, last week, yesterday, a month ago

In 2014, Asimo played football with a US president.

2 A finished indefinite point in time: when she was a child, a long time ago, the other day

Scientists created Asimo **a long time ago** in order to help people in need.

Regular verbs are formed by adding -ed, -d or ied: start**ed,** creat**ed**, carr**ied**

Irregular verbs **do not** follow a rule. Some are also difficult to spell.

have – **had** be – **was/were** become – **became** take – **took**

Focus

1 **Find out about the history of the telephone. Complete the text with verbs in the past simple.**

Alexander Graham Bell is known for inventing the telephone in the late 1800s. He [1] was (be) born in Scotland in 1847 and [2] ______ (become) interested in the science of sound because both his mother and wife [3] ______ (be) deaf. He loved doing experiments and eventually he was able to send voice signals down a telephone wire.

The first telephone call [4] ______ (take) place in March 1876 between Alexander Graham Bell and his assistant Thomas Watson. The telephone he [5] ______ (use) was tall and long and you [6] ______ (have) to use a separate mouth and ear piece, one to listen and one to speak. As design developed people [7] ______ (begin) to use a round dial with numbers. Now we use wireless phones, which let us talk and move around the house at the same time.

Practice

2 **Complete the text about the evolution of the mobile telephone. Use verbs in the word box.**

~~make~~	carry	run	cost
change	weigh	not be	

> **Get it right!**
>
> Don't use the present simple to talk about past events.
>
> In the 1990s people ~~begin~~ began to use mobile phones.

A Motorola employee called Dr Martin Cooper [1] ___made___ the first ever mobile telephone call in 1973. The first mobiles had huge handsets that could only be used in cars. They [2] __________ nearly $2000 and the battery [3] __________ out after 20 minutes.

In the 1980s, only wealthy people [4] __________ mobiles around with them and they were extremely heavy! They [5] __________ almost a kilo and connections [6] __________ reliable.

In the 1990s, people used smaller, lighter phones and the new 2G network [7] __________ the way people communicated through text and picture messages. Phones changed in design too, from the 'slider' phone to 'flip top' ones.

Decades later we have slim, light smartphones with touch screens. They have high definition, mega-pixel cameras that take great photos and selfies too!

Challenge

3 **Ask a parent or an older person in your family about their first mobile phone. When did they get it? What was it like? What functions did it have?**

Write a short paragraph about it.

____

____

____

____

4.3 *Will* for future predictions

Use of English

We can use ***will*** to make predictions about the future. For the negative, we can say ***will not*** or ***won't***.

I **will** be a scientist

We'**ll** all have electric cars.

Cities **won't** be as polluted.

Will people ride electric bikes more?

Focus

1 **Dimitri is giving a presentation about a new invention called the Brain Pen. Order the words to make five questions you could ask him.**

1 change / Brain Pen / will / what / the / ?

What will the Brain Pen change?

2 will / save / it / how / time / ?

____

3 get / how / power / its / will / it / ?

____

4 it / what / do / will / ?

____

5 connected / what / be / will / the Brain Pen / to / ?

____

Get it right!

Will does not need 'to' after it.

I think this **will to be** an amazing invention for the classroom.

Practice

2 **Now complete Dimitri's presentation with *will* or *won't* and a verb from the box.**

be	connect	~~change~~	write	help	not have to	like	read	improve

A Hello everyone, today I'm going to describe my idea for an incredible invention. It [1] will change the way we do our homework and it [2]__________ our schoolwork and exam results too!

B The Brain Pen [3]__________ powered by your brainwaves. You [4]__________ hold it – you just think about what you want to put on the paper and it [5]__________ for you! It can go as fast or as slow as you want it to.

C It [6]__________ to headphones and the pads on the side of your head [7]__________ your thoughts and these will be transmitted to your pen, which will write them down.

D To sum up, I think both kids and adults [8]__________ my idea. Nowadays we spend a lot of time typing on keyboards, so this invention [9]__________ you write quickly when you have to write by hand.

3 **Match the questions in Activity 1 to the correct paragraph in Activity 2. There is more than one question for one of the paragraphs! Write the answers to the questions in your notebook.**

Question:

1 A It will change the way we do out homework.

2 ______ 3 ______ 4 ______

Challenge

4 **Describe an invention that you think your school will need in the future. Draw a picture in your notebook to show your idea.**

4.4 Changing the world

1 **Read Kim's essay about an important invention. Put the sentences a–f in the correct place to complete it.**

[1] ___b___ If we didn't have television, we wouldn't know about important things happening in our country or the world. [2] ________. **For example**, when we watch the news, we can find out about what is happening in the next town or on the other side of the world, all in one programme. [3] ________.

I think that television is important to educate us and entertain us too. There are educational TV programmes [4] ________. Television gives us important information but it also makes us relax and laugh too. We can watch TV for fun, [5] ________. But some people say that families would talk to each other more if there was no television. **In my opinion**, families can make time for talking, going out and also watching TV together too. [6] ________.

a **such as** documentaries about wildlife, history and culture.

b **In my opinion**, one of the most important inventions of all time is the television.

c **This means that** we can know more information about our own country and other countries too.

d **for example**, when we watch cartoons and movies that tell great stories.

e **For these reasons, I think that** TV is one of the most important inventions.

f **This is because** television can bring us pictures and information very quickly and from far away.

2 **Write the phrases in bold from the essay that we use for giving examples and opinions in the correct column.**

Giving examples	Giving reasons/opinions
For example	I think that

3 **What is the best invention of the past 10 years?**
Choose one of these examples or think of your own.

The drone

The tablet

The LED light bulb

In my opinion the LED light bulb is the best invention of the past 10 years.

4 **Write two or three reasons to support your opinion here.**

a because it uses less electricity.

b ______

c ______

5 **Now write your essay in your notebook. Draw a picture of the invention too.**

- Use Kim's essay to help you.
- Use your notes in Activity 4.
- Use phrases for giving opinions, reasons and examples.

4.5 Start Small, Think Big

1 **Read the extract again from the story *Start Small, Think Big*. Put the sentences about the story in the correct order.**

a Suddenly Garth sees the Barker Boys walking towards him and he tries to run away. ______

b Garth feels very excited about testing his new invention – his Bodybrella – outside in the street near his home. __1__

c The Barker Boys laugh at Garth and his Bodybrella. ______

d The lady has an idea to organise a young inventors' competition for the town. ______

e After talking to the lady, Garth feels much better. ______

f A lady from another house in Garth's street has seen Garth and the boys and asks him if he is alright. ______

g Garth is pleased that his Bodybrella protects him against the rain and wind. ______

h Then the lady looks at Garth's Bodybrella and likes it a lot. She thinks that it is a clever idea. ______

i Garth feels very upset. Now he thinks that his invention is a failure. ______

j Todd Barker throws the Bodybrella over his shoulder. The boys run away laughing. ______

2 **Change the adjectives into adverbs. Then use them to complete the sentences.**

~~careful~~	secure	quick	rough	gentle

a Garth didn't want to damage the Bodybrella so he put it on carefully.

b He fastened it ____________ with the strap under his chin.

c When he saw the boys, Garth turned around ____________ to run home.

d Todd Barker pulled the Bodybrella ____________ off Garth's body.

e The lady took the Bodybrella ____________ from Garth because she could see it was damaged.

3 **Match the sentence halves.**

1 Have you tried ...

2 When I picked ...

3 She stood on the winners' podium and held

4 They ran ...

a up my book, there was a spider under it.

b up the trophy proudly.

c out that new video game yet?

d back home quickly to miss the rain.

4 Values: **Believe in yourself!**

Imagine you're going to try something new and you're feeling a bit nervous. Tick (✓) the attitudes that are the most helpful.

a If other kids can do it, so can I! ☐

b If I can't do it, everyone will laugh at me. ☐

c If I don't try, I won't know if I can do it. ☐

d If I fail, I'll feel really bad! ☐

e If I know I've tried my best, I'll feel OK. ☐

4.6 Check your progress

Choose the correct answer and write it in the space.

1 A __________ is a two-wheeled, electric gadget.
   a mountain bike   b tablet   c hoverboard

2 A __________ is an instrument that you use for finding directions.
   a compass   b zip   c smartphone

3 A Japanese company __________ Asimo to the world in 2000.
   a started   b presented   c developed

4 I really __________ the exhibition yesterday.
   a enjoyed   b enjoy   c will enjoy

5 Pandemics __________ the way we live in the future.
   a changed   b will to change   c will change

6 You __________ to put petrol in your electric car.
   a will   b won't need   c won't to need

7 Have you __________ your latest invention yet?
   a tried on   b tried back   c tried out

8 It was very fragile, so he put it __________ on the table.
   a roughly   b carefully   c quickly

9 __________, the most important invention in the world is the internet.
   a This means that   b In my opinion   c Because of ...

10 Programmes __________ documentaries and police dramas are really interesting.
   a because   b for example   c such as

4.7 Reflection

Think about what you have studied in this unit. Answer the questions.

1 What topics did you like and why?

____

____

2 What activities did you like and why?

____

____

3 What did you find challenging and why?

____

____

4 What help do you need now?

____

____

5 What do you want to find out more about?

____

____

5 Money

5.1 Spending a sum of money

1 Vocabulary: **Can you find and circle six words or phrases in the word snake?**

2 **Use the words in Activity 1 to complete the sentences.**

a That ____________ helps a lot of people in our country.

b It's an expensive ____________, but everyone wants to wear their trainers!

c That T-shirt is new and you want to throw it away! What a ____________!

d The phone is very cheap – is it made to ____________ or will it break in a few months?

e I can't ____________ to buy that hoodie – I haven't got enough money.

f If you ____________ your pocket money, you'll be able to buy that video game.

3 **Think and write your own examples of ...**

a Something you would buy if you could **afford** it: ____________

If I could afford it, I'd buy a helicopter!

b A popular **brand** in your country: ____________

c A **charity** in your country: ____________

d Something you have that has **lasted** a long time: ____________

e Somewhere you can put money you have **saved**: ____________

f Something you think is a **waste of money**: ____________

4 **Read the saving tips. Can you match each one to a picture?**

1 **Watch your money grow!** Save your pocket money in a clear glass jar.

2 **Have three money jars.** Divide your pocket money:
1 Spend (small things); 2 Save (bigger things); 3 Give (helping others).

3 **Think before you buy!** Ask yourself, 'Do I really want this?'

4 **Set a savings goal,** to help you save for something big.

5 **Start a savings diary.** Trying to save but can't? Write down what you spend and think about where you can save that money instead!

a 

b 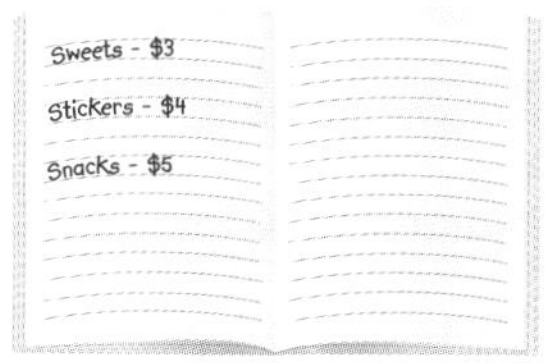

c 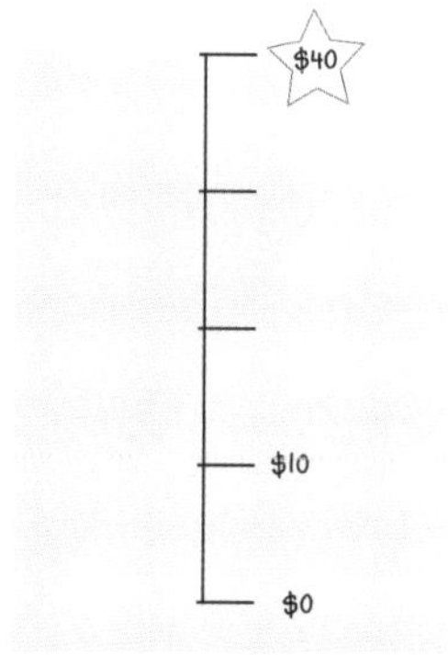

d 

e 

5 **Read again and tick (✓) the tips that you (or someone in your family) have tried. Which ideas do you like best?**

Challenge

6 **Imagine you have $50! You are going to divide it up into three jars, *Spend*, *Save* and *Give* (point 2 in Activity 4). Decide how much money to put in each jar and explain your decisions here.**

I'm going to put $20 in the **Save** jar because ...

I'll put $10 in the **Give** jar for the Animal Rescue charity, because ...

5.2 Comparative and superlative adverbs

Use of English

We can use **comparative adverbs** to show change or compare how something is done.

He **grows out** of them **less quickly** than me.
She **works harder** than everyone else.

We can also use **superlative adverbs** to make comparisons.

I **spend** my pocket money **fastest** in the shopping mall!
We **go** shopping **most often** at the weekend.

To make a superlative adverb stronger, we often use *the* + superlative adverb.

This brand of sportswear always **sells the best** because it **lasts the longest**.

Base adverb	Comparative	Superlative
1 syllable: fast, hard	fast**er**, hard**er**	(the) fast**est**, (the) hard**est**
2 syllables: quickly, often	**more / less** quickly **more / less** often	(the) **most / least** quickly (the) **most / least** often
Irregular: well, badly	**better**, **worse**	(the) **best**, (the) **worst**

Focus

1 **The Ruiz family have saved and bought a camper van for holidays. Read and circle the correct words in the sentences.**

a In the family, who saved **the hardest / most hard**?

b Mateo thinks he saved his money the **most quickly / quickliest**.

c He's right! In the family, Lucas spends money the **more fast / fastest!**

d Now, with the camper van, they can all go on holiday **more / most** cheaply.

e So they can have holidays **more often / oftener** than before.

f And in the van, they can travel **more / least** comfortably than before.

Practice

2 **Kofi has saved his pocket money and wants to buy a new football shirt. Circle and number the six errors in the conversation, then write the corrections at the end.**

Kofi: There's the City shirt and the National kit. I don't know which one to buy!

Dad: Well, which one will you wear the oftenest, do you think? 1

Kofi: The City shirt, because we go to City games all the time … but I like the National shirt more better!

Dad: OK, but I think that shirt costs much than the other one. Have you checked?

Kofi: Oh yes, it's more expensive. I think I've got enough pocket money …

Dad: OK then, try them both on. Let's see which one fits better.

Kofi: The National shirt definitely fits the best but it costs the more! I don't know what to do!

Dad: Mmm … and the City shirt is a bit too big – it fits looser, but that is a good thing because you are growing more faster this year than ever before!

Kofi: So the City shirt will last the most longest?

1 most often 4 ______

2 ______ 5 ______

3 ______ 6 ______

Get it right!

Remember to use the correct form of the adverb.

~~See you late~~. See you **later**.

My sister can sing ~~more better~~ **better** than my brother.

Challenge

3 **Can you complete the questions with the correct adverb? Then answer the questions.**

more often	more easily	best

a Do you save your pocket money? How can you save it ______?

b What do you like doing ______? Buying something nice or going out somewhere exciting? Which is the most fun?

c What do you do ______? Go shopping or play sports? How many times a month?

5.3 Quantifiers

Use of English

We use the **quantifiers**, *several* and *plenty of*, to describe amounts of things (we don't know exactly how much).

At the school fair, there were **several** book stalls ... (*several* = 3 or 4)
... and there were **plenty of** food stalls ... (*plenty of* = lots of)

Either ... or and *both of* always refer to 'two'.
Either ... or means a choice of two.

both or *both of* = two people or things

Both comes after the verb, *to be*; but before other verbs:

You are **both** very good at helping ...
We **both** baked cakes for the school fair.
You can **either** help with the book stall **or** tidy up the rubbish – it's up to you!

neither ... nor – the negative form of *either ... or* ('not either')

There are **neither** burgers **nor** sausages at the school fair – most of the food is vegetarian.

Focus

1 **Sara and Dani have a food stall at the school fair. Look at the picture. Is each sentence true or false? Correct the false sentences in your notebooks.**

a There are **several** types of drink for sale. ______

b **Neither** Sara **nor** Dani are helping on the food stall. ______

c There are **plenty of** cakes for sale. ______

d You can buy **either** sandwiches **or** water on the stall. ______

e **Both of** the children are pouring fruit drinks. ______

Practice

2 **Read Sara and Dani's report about their food stall. Choose the correct quantifiers to complete their report.**

several	neither ... nor	either ... or	both of	plenty of

Get it right!

Remember to use correct word order with both.

~~We both are helping~~
We **are both** helping on the stall.
~~We want both to go~~
We **both want** to go to the school fair.

We had a very good day at the school fair! We sold all our cupcakes and all our fruit juice by 12 p.m. So, we didn't have to work in the afternoon – we had 1 ____________ time to relax and enjoy the rest of the fair.

There were 2 ____________ food and drink stalls at the fair – maybe about three or four different ones. On most of the stalls, people could buy 3 ____________ food ____________ a drink – but not food and drink together. But on our stall, people could buy something to eat AND drink, so maybe that is the reason that our stall was so popular!

We had a great day! 4 ____________ of us got bored ____________ wanted to go home early! 5 ____________ us want to do another stall at the next school fair!

Challenge

3 **Lexi and Jack had a stall with different things at the school fair. Can you write sentences to describe the picture? Include at least three quantifiers (more if you can!).**

Both of the children look happy.

____

____

____

____

5.4 The question of pocket money

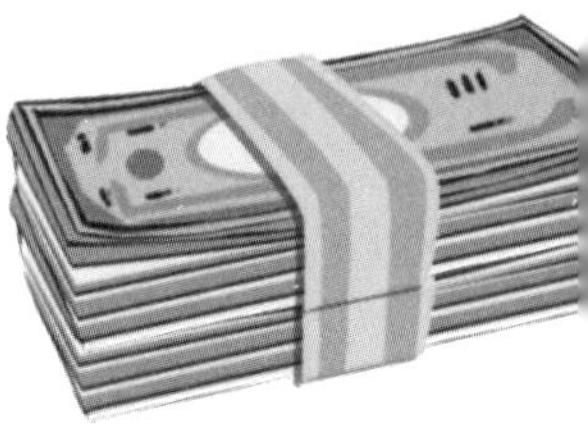

1 **Read Dana's essay and choose a sentence, a–d, to complete the missing parts.**

Does a lot of money make us happy?

1__________ **In my opinion**, money is important **but** there are other things that are more important than having a lot of money.

2__________ **because** we can't do anything or go anywhere if we aren't healthy. If you have a lot of money, you can buy nice things for yourself and travel to exciting places. **But** you can't enjoy these things if you don't feel healthy.

3__________ Some people are very rich, but don't have any good friends and I think that's a sad situation. **However**, if you can afford to do lots of hobbies, you will meet a lot of new people **and** maybe make some new friends. **But** if you are very rich, how do you know if your new friends really like you or your money?

4__________ **but** there are other things that are more important than lots of money. **Therefore**, I would like to say that good health and good family and friends are more important than being very rich!

a **Secondly**, it is more important to have a good family and good friends.

b A lot of people think that we need to have a large amount of money to make us happy.

c **Finally**, I think it is important to have money for the things we need.

d **Firstly**, it is more important to be healthy.

Writing tip

Connecting words

Use **connecting words** to organise your ideas logically and help readers follow the points in your essay.

Firstly, when you have pocket money you ...

... pocket money is a good idea **because** it teaches us to manage money ourselves.

2 **Read Dana's essay again and answer the questions in your notebook. Use the connecting words in bold to help you.**

a What is the main opinion of the essay?

b Which two points support the main opinion?

c Find one point against the main opinion.

d In which paragraph can you find a summary of the main points?

3 **Do you agree with Dana's points? Think of two more points to add to the essay (you can either agree or disagree!).**

____

____

4 **Choose a reflexive pronoun to complete the sentences.**

himself	**herself**
ourselves	**yourselves**
themselves	**itself**

a My brother earned his extra pocket money __________ by doing jobs at home.

b Dad bought Kris and Jan one video game and they bought the other one __________.

c To save money, my sister repaired her bike __________.

d Why are you still feeding the kitten? It can feed __________ now.

e My brother and I painted our bedroom __________.

f If you both want such expensive phones, you must save some of the money __________.

5 **Write a short essay for this title: *How much pocket money do you need at your age*? Plan it like this:**

- What is your opinion or point of view? Write points to support your opinion. Write at least one contrasting point.
- Organise your points under these headings:
  - ***Introduction to the main point of view (what is the essay about?)***
  - ***Points to support the main opinion***
  - ***One point against the main opinion***
  - ***Conclusion: summarises the main point***
- Remember to use connecting words!

5.5 Billionaire Boy

1 **How much is one billion? Tick (✓) the correct answer.**

a 100 x 1 million ☐ b 1 000 x 1 million ☐

2 **How do you write one billion in numbers? Tick (✓) the correct answer.**

a 100 000 000 ☐ b 1 000 000 000 ☐

3 **Read the story again. Are the sentences true or false? Correct the false sentences in your notebook.**

a Joe's house is so big that he only knows part of it. ____________

b He has only lived in his house for a very short time. ____________

c The carpets are made of wool. ____________

d Joe is happy with the cheque his father gave him for his birthday. ____________

e Joe wants to have his own speedboat as a present too. ____________

f Joe wants to go to a different school. ____________

g His dad doesn't want him to go to the local free state school. ____________

h He thinks the other children at the new school will be unkind to Joe. ____________

i Mr Spud refuses to let Joe go to the new school. ____________

4 **What is the reason that Joe wants to go to a new school? Do you think he will find what he is looking for? Why? Why not?**

____

____

____

5 **Remember the money idioms from Lesson 5? Choose the correct words to complete the idioms. Can you match each one to a definition?**

burn	money	job

1 He has more ____________ than sense. ________

2 He has a ____________ that pays peanuts. ________

3 He has money to ____________. ________

a A job that doesn't pay very much money.

b When someone has more money than they need or they spend their money on things that are unnecessary.

c When someone has a lot of money but isn't clever enough to spend it wisely.

Challenge

6 **Values: One of your family has given you $20 US to give away to a charity or someone else that needs it.**

- First, find out how much $20 US is in the currency of your country.
- What are you going to do with it? Write your ideas and reasons in your notebook and draw a picture to represent your idea.

I'm going to give it to ... because ...

____

____

____

____

____

____

____

____

____

____

5.6 Check your progress

1 **Read the clues and write the words in the word puzzle. Find the hidden word!**

1 A synonym of *real*.
2 A connecting word that introduces a second point.
3 An organisation that helps people in need.
4 A synonym of *false*.
5 To keep money for the future.
6 A connecting word that shows contrast.
7 You can spend or save this.
8 When you have enough money to buy something.
9 In my ... (your point of view)
10 A connecting word to give a reason.
11 A connecting word that introduces the first point.

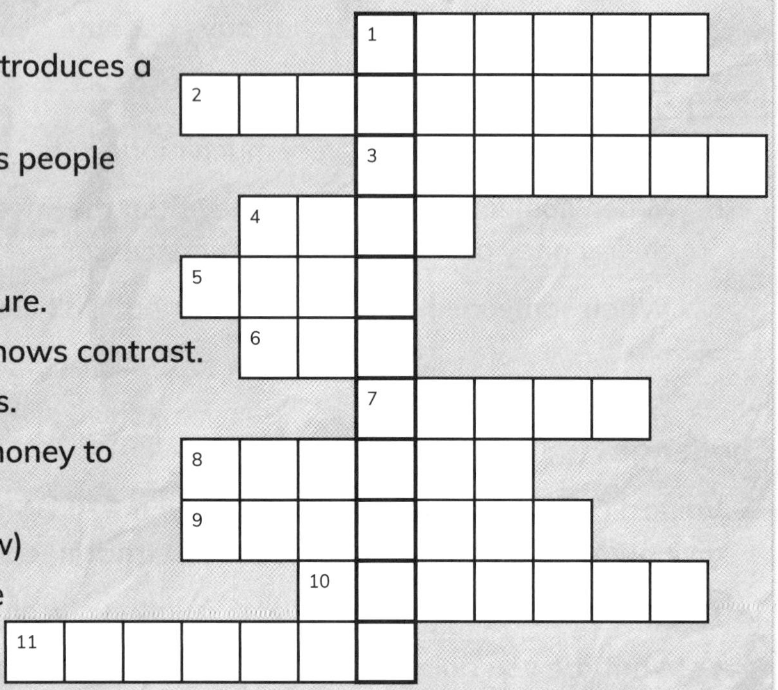

Which word is hidden in the puzzle? ____________

2 **Remember the class discussion in Lesson 5.3? Choose the correct word to complete the advice.**

A class discussion can be fun and interesting. [1] **However / Finally**, there are some basic rules. Keep the discussion [2] **formal / informal** so everyone feels comfortable and wants to participate. An informal discussion still needs to be [3] **polite / aggressive** – make sure you listen and wait your turn, then everyone can make their points more [4] **easily / easilier**. [5] **Neither / Several** people shouldn't speak at the same time. Respond to each other's opinions [6] **and / therefore** don't be [7] **rude / friendly** or aggressive if you disagree. You can still be [8] **friendly / rude** and respectful, even if you don't share your classmates' opinions.

5.7 Reflection

Think about what you have studied in this unit. Answer the questions.

1 What topics did you like and why?

2 What activities did you like and why?

3 What did you find challenging and why?

4 What help do you need now?

5 What do you want to find out more about?

6 People and work

6.1 How do you get a job?

1 **Vocabulary: Jobs**

Complete the sentences with the correct adjective. Use the jumbled letters to help you.

a opmurcte gmporaemrr __ __ __ __ __ __ __ __   __ __ __ __ __ __ __ __ __ __
A person who writes instructions that a computer can understand.

b cnsieec ectaehr __ __ __ __ __ __ __   __ __ __ __ __ __ __
A person who teaches physics, chemistry and biology.

c tpspyisohherait __ __ __ __ __ __ __ __ __ __ __ __ __ __ __
A person who treats sports injuries.

d nairem goliositb __ __ __ __ __ __   __ __ __ __ __ __ __ __ __
A scientist who studies sea wildlife.

e tve __ __ __ An animal doctor.

f egnernie __ __ __ __ __ __ __ __
A person who designs machines and structures for buildings.

2 **Can you find three compound nouns in the word puzzles in Activity 1?**

Write the nouns here. ______________ ______________ ______________

3 **Complete the sentences with these compound nouns.**

university degree
work experience
voluntary work

a My older sister does ______________ for an animal charity in her school holidays.

b For some jobs, you need to study for a ______________ first.

c When you do ______________, you work in a company for a short time while you are still at school or university.

4 **Do you know anyone who has done *work experience*, a *university degree* or *voluntary work*? If so, write two interesting facts in your notebook.**

My brother is studying for a university degree in ...

5 **Read the interview with Deepak. Which job in Activity 1 does he do?**

____

Interviewer: [1] What's your job?

Deepak: I'm a _____________ at a city high school.

Interviewer: [2] _____________

Deepak: Well, I was always really keen on science in school, and I wanted to help children understand and enjoy it like I did.

Interviewer: [3] _____________

Deepak: Yes, overall I think I am good at what I do. I'm quite good with kids in general. I understand the way they think and learn, so teaching is the perfect job for me.

Interviewer: [4] _____________

Deepak: I got a university degree – you need to study hard and know your subject very well if you want to teach it to other people. Then after that I studied for an extra year to become a teacher. I did a lot of work experience in a school, teaching real classes.

Interviewer: [5] _____________

Deepak: My favourite thing is when my students get excited about what they are learning. For example, when we do a science experiment, and everyone has fun and learns something new at the same time.

6 **Read the interview again. Match the questions to the answers (2–5) in Activity 5.**

a What do you enjoy most about your job?

b Why did you choose this job?

c What's your job?

d Do you think you are good at your job? Why?

e What did you do to get your job?

Challenge

7 **In your notebook, write the name of a job that you find interesting. Write two questions to ask someone who does that job. Then imagine and write their answers.**

6.2 Adjectives + prepositions + nouns

Use of English

Some **adjectives** and **prepositions** always go together.
There are no fixed rules, so it helps to learn the words together, as a 'chunk'.
Adjective + preposition phrases are often followed by a **noun** (or pronoun).

Here are some patterns to help you remember (but remember that there are exceptions).

We use (adjective +) *at*, for skills and abilities.

I was **good at** maths and science anyway. I **worked hard** at them at school.

We use *about* and *of* to talk about feelings.

Ben is **nervous about** his maths exam. Hua is **proud of** her science project.

We can also use adjectives with *in* and *with*.

For this job, you need to be **experienced in** photography.
He is **great with** engines and machines.

Focus

1 **Read about Lisa, a chocolate expert. Circle the correct prepositions.**

Lisa Tomas is a chocolate expert! She is **fascinated** [1] **in / by** chocolate and she wants other people to get **excited** [2] **about / at** it too. She works for a famous chocolate brand and sells their products to shops and hotels. To do Lisa's job, you must be very **enthusiastic** [3] **about / in** the product because you have to persuade people to buy it! You must be **good** [4] **of / with** people and enjoy talking to them about the different types of chocolate.

As a child, Lisa was very **fond** [5] **of / in** desserts and she loved cooking and baking. When she was a teenager, she tried making her own chocolate (not easy!). She soon realised that she was more **interested** [6] **with / in** chocolate than any other sweet treat and she decided then that she wanted to become a chocolate expert!

2 **Underline the noun or pronoun that follows each *adjective + preposition* phrase.**

Get it right!

Remember to use the correct preposition after the adjective.

We are so happy ~~for~~ **about** our exam results!
I am so angry ~~to~~ **with** you!

Practice

3 **Choose the correct prepositions to complete the dialogue about Tom's job. You will need to use some of the words twice.**

on	about	in	at	by

Interviewer: Hi everyone! Welcome to Job Spot, the podcast that looks at fun and unusual jobs. If you like a great day out and you're **keen** [1] ________ theme parks, our next guest can tell you a thing or two! Welcome Tom! Tell us about your job.

Tom: Hello. I work in theme parks, testing water slides and rollercoaster rides!

Interviewer: Wow! Sounds amazing. You must get very **excited** [2] ________ your work!

Tom: Yes, I do. I'm **crazy** [3] ________ it. But there is a serious side to it. I test the rides to make sure they are safe for families to use.

Interviewer: So, what kind of things do you look for when you test the rides?

Tom: For the water slides, I'm **interested** [4] ________ the height, speed and the amount of water. All these things affect the safety of the slide. You need to be **good** [5] ________ maths and science in my job, so you can understand how things are built and what happens when people use them.

Interviewer: So did you work **hard** [6] ________ those subjects when you were at school?

Tom: Yes, I did, I was always **fascinated** [7] ________ machines and how they worked, so that interest helped me to study the school subjects – and get my dream job today!

Challenge

4 **Make true sentences about you and your family and friends. Use the adjectives below. Remember to add the correct preposition!**

keen	fascinated	fond
interested	crazy	good

My best friend is crazy about ... ________________

I'm quite good at ... ________________

6.3 Reported speech

Use of English

We use **reported speech** to tell someone what another person has said.

In reported statements, the verb tense often moves further back from the tense in the direct statements.

Direct speech	Reported speech
'I often **do** experiments in space,' Karina said.	**Karina said that she** often **did** experiments in space.
'How **are you preparing** for the space journey?' they asked.	**They asked** how **we were preparing** for the space journey.
'Astronauts **will** explore Mars in the future,' she said.	**She said that astronauts would** explore Mars in the future.
Direct commands '**Wear** protective clothing'	**He told them to wear** protective clothing.

Focus

1 **American astronaut Karina is talking to Year 6 students. Can you complete her reported statements with the correct verbs and forms?**

My spacesuit can do so many things! It supplies oxygen for me to breathe when I'm in space. It also has air conditioning and heating, to protect me from the heat and cold. My space suit even provides water for me to drink. It's very big and heavy – it takes me one hour to put it on! Maybe in the future they will invent a lighter space suit!'

a She told the students that the space suit __________ her from heat and cold.

b She said that the space suit __________ water for her to drink.

c She __________ them that the space suit was heavy to wear.

d She hoped that they __________ invent a lighter space suit in the future.

Get it right!

Remember the pronoun with 'tell'.

~~She told that her school has a uniform.~~ She told **me** that her school has a uniform.

~~He told to put on our jackets.~~ He told **us** to put on our jackets.

Remember: there is no pronoun after 'say' ~~Karina said us that she ....~~ Karina **said** that she couldn't put her spacesuit on quickly.

Practice

2 **Read Bao's ideas for changing the design of the kit at his school running club. Can you complete the table with direct and reported statements?**

Direct statement / command	Reported statement / command
'I want to make some changes to the sports kit.'	1 He said that he wanted to make some changes to the sports kit.
2 ________________	He said we needed a brighter stripe on the t-shirt.
'A brighter stripe will be easier to see at night.'	3 ________________
'It isn't easy to see the school logo on our sports kit'.	4 ________________
'Put the school logo at the top of the sleeve.'	5 He told ________________
'People can see a logo better at the top of the sleeve, near the shoulder.'	6 He told ________________
7 ________________	He explained that the backpack didn't have any pockets.

Challenge

3 **Write three questions to ask your favourite famous person or sports star. Imagine his/her answers. Write the answers in reported statements in your notebook.**

I asked ...., who is a famous .... about .... She said that ....

6.4 Let's get a job!

1 **Read the first lines of the job advertisements. Match each one with a picture.**

1 We are looking for a funny actor to star in our comedy play. ________

2 We are looking for a talented hairdresser to join our creative team. ________

3 We are looking for a dynamic pilot to fly a huge jet plane. ________

> **Writing tip**
>
> **Use shortened sentences in adverts**
>
> ~~You~~ Must be able to do experiments. Experience needed ...

2 **Match the lines from the rest of the job adverts with the correct jobs in Activity 1.**

1 Must be an expert at using a pair of scissors. ___a___

2 Must be knowledgeable about humorous books and plays. ________

3 Must know how all the controls in a plane work. ________

4 Interviews will be held in the theatre. ________

5 Experience needed – our customers want to look good! ________

6 Must be able to make people laugh a lot. ________

7 Interviews will be held in the plane. ________

8 Interviews will be held in the salon. ________

9 Must know how to fly across the world in the right direction. ________

10 Must look good in funny costumes. ________

11 Must have good eyesight so you don't cut the wrong bit. ________

12 Must be good with heights. ________

3 **Read the Use of English box. Can you complete the sentences with the correct forms of the verbs?**

work	practise	do
send	~~study~~	not look

Use of English

Present continuous review

We use the present continuous to describe continuous actions happening now.

We ***are looking*** *for a friendly zookeeper …*
They ***are recruiting*** *genius-level inventors …*

a Right now my sister is studying for a university degree.

b I ____________ you an email about the job now – look out for it in your inbox.

c ____________ your older brother still ____________ for that famous sports brand?

d My cousins ____________ work experience at a technology company.

e No, he ____________ for a job yet – he is still studying.

f Thea wants to be a musician when she grows up, so she ____________ hard at the moment.

4 **Write sentences in your notebook about what you are doing at the moment. Use the present continuous.**

a Describe a school project you're working on at the moment.

b What's happening in the place you are in right now?

c Describe an activity you're doing at the moment.

Challenge

5 **Complete the job advert with your own ideas.**

- We are looking for a (adjective) and (adjective) (job title)
- Experience need – (why?) ____________
- Must be good at … (?) ____________
- Must be knowledgeable about … (?) ____________
- Must be interested in … (?) ____________
- Interviews will be held in the … (where?) ____________

6.5 You can be anything

1 **Read the poem *You can be anything* by Teri Hopkins on pages 102–103 in the Learner's Book again. Tick (✓) the sentences that express the advice in the poem.**

a There are lots of different types of jobs that you can do. ✓

b You can be anything you want to be – you don't have to work hard. ☐

c It is possible to do any kind of job, but you must make an effort. ☐

d You should make goals for yourself and aim high. ☐

e If something goes wrong, you should keep trying. ☐

f If you are happy in the job you do, you will be successful. ☐

g Someone else will decide the job you do in the future. ☐

h You are responsible for choosing the job you do in the future. ☐

2 Word study: **Suffixes**

Add -ist / -er / -or to complete the words for jobs.
Then circle the jobs that appear in the poem.

scient ist	flor ______	firefight ______
doct ______	teach ______	police office ______
dent ______	build ______	hairdress ______
art ______	sing ______	act ______
plaster ______		

3 **What are their jobs? Use the words in Activity 2 to help you.**

a  ______________

b 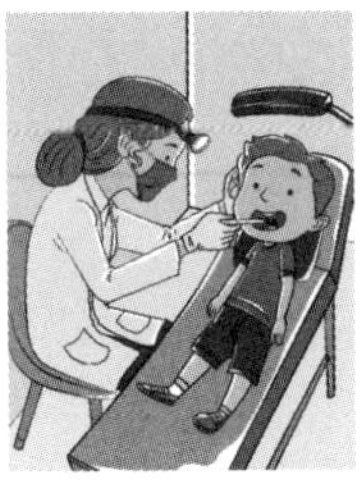 ______________

c  ______________

d  ______________

4 **What jobs could these children have when they grow up? Write a sentence with *could* after each description.**

> **Language focus: could (+verb)**
>
> In these sentences, we use *could* (+ verb) to talk about something that is possible.
>
> You **could be** a doctor and look after the sick.
>
> We use *couldn't* (+ verb) to talk about something that isn't possible.
>
> She **couldn't learn** to drive – she isn't old enough.

a Freya is good at science and interested in helping other people.
She could ____________________.

b Jian is great at making and fixing things.
He ____________________.

c Marta is creative and fond of growing plants.
She ____________________.

d Dmitri is crazy about music and has a strong voice.
He ____________________.

e Tara is keen on maths and good with children.
She ____________________.

f Marco is scared of fire and doesn't like heights.
He couldn't ____________________.

5 **Now complete the sentences to make them true for you.**

a If I work hard, I ____________________.

b When I grow up, I ____________________.

c If my family move house, we ____________________.

d If I finish my homework early, I ____________________.

e If I meet my friends this weekend, we ____________________.

6 Values: **Working hard and setting goals**
Look at the children's goals. Match goals 1–3 to the advice a–c.

1 Elena wants to be in the Under-12 basketball team for her school.

2 Theo wants to save up for a new bike.

3 Chao wants to get a good grade in his Maths exam.

a You should do two hours of extra study each weekend

b You should do more jobs at home to earn extra pocket money.

c You should do half an hour of extra net practice a day.

6.6 Check your progress

1 **Can you solve the crossword puzzle? Read the clues to find the missing words.**

Across →

1 A design used by a company to promote its products.

5 A performer who does difficult gymnastics to entertain people.

6 You use this to fasten your jeans or back pack.

7 This adjective describes doing something that can be dangerous.

9 This person creates food dishes in hotels and restaurants.

10 This person looks after sick people in hospital.

Down ↓

2 This strong force makes things fall to the ground.

3 This adjective means 'in good physical condition'.

4 This adjective is the opposite of 'shy'.

8 This part of your clothing covers the arms.

Challenge

2 **Make a revision crossword to test your friends.**

6.7 Reflection

Think about what you have studied in this unit. Answer the questions.

1 What topics did you like and why?

2 What activities did you like and why?

3 What did you find challenging and why?

4 What help do you need now?

5 What do you want to find out more about?

7 Nature's power

7.1 The power of volcanoes

1 **Vocabulary: Volcanoes**

Choose the correct words to label the diagram.

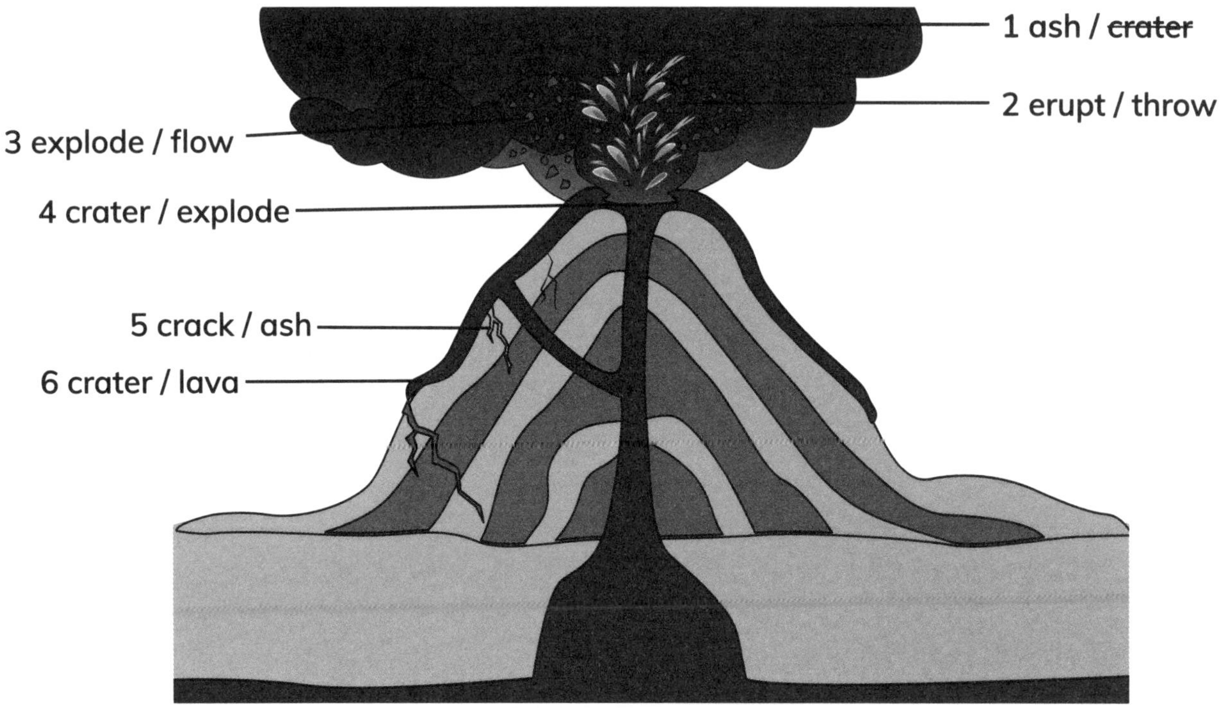

2 **Complete the sentences about the volcano diagram with the words in Activity 1.**

a Red hot ______________ flows down the side of the volcano.

b The flowing lava is so hot that it makes ______________ on the volcano's surface.

c The molten rock (magma) comes out of the ______________ at the top.

d When the volcano ______________, lava and a cloud of smoke come out of the top.

e This cloud of smoke is called an ______________ cloud.

f When pressure builds, this cloud can ______________ 30 km into the air!

3 **What happened at Mount Pinatubo? Read the text to find out and complete the text with the correct form of the verbs in the word box.**

cause	~~erupted~~	explode	die
release	lose	cover	

In 1991, Mount Pinatubo in the Philippines [1] <u>erupted</u>. The eruption was huge. The **magma** inside the volcano travelled to the surface and [2] ________ **violently**, throwing enormous areas of lava down the sides of the mountain in huge **avalanches**. The explosion [3] ________ an ash cloud to rise over 30 kilometres into the air. The eruption [4] ________ the countryside around the volcano in an enormous blanket of ash and smoke.

The eruption had a **catastrophic** effect on the people living nearby. Hundreds of people [5] ________ in the explosion and thousands of people [6] ________ their homes.

In the three months before the eruption happened, the volcano gave **warnings** that it was going to explode. Molten rock rose 32 kilometres from deep in the Earth and caused small earthquakes. There were also steam explosions that destroyed three craters on the north side of the volcano and [7] ________ **poisonous** gases into the air.

4 **Read again. Match the words in bold from Activity 3 to the definitions.**

a Large amounts of rock and lava falling down. ________

b Very hot melted rock inside the volcano. ________

c Signs that something bad is going to happen. ________

d Very harmful and dangerous to health. ________

e Causing great disaster and destruction. ________

f With great force that causes harm. ________

5 **Which facts about Mount Pinatubo did you think were the most interesting or surprising? Write your answer in your notebook.**

Challenge

6 **What other things would you like to find out about volcanoes? Write two (or more) questions; then look for the answers online or in the library.**

7.2 Past simple and past continuous

Use of English

We use the **past continuous** to describe actions happening at the same time as another action in the past. The other action is usually in the **past simple**.

We were making a film in Indonesia **when** the volcano suddenly exploded.

We make the **past continuous** with the past form of the verb, *be* (*was* / *were*) + verb + *-ing*. We can use linking words, ***when***, ***as***, ***while***.

While everything seemed normal outside, magma was rising inside the volcano.

People were escaping from their homes **as** the volcano erupted.

We make the negative form with *wasn't* / *weren't* (*was* / *were not*).

I **wasn't playing** in the park when the lightning struck, I was at home.

Luckily we **weren't standing** too close when the explosion happened.

Questions

Where were you **going** when you saw the ash cloud?

Was she **working** nearby while the eruption happened? **Yes**, he was / **No**, he wasn't.

Focus

1 **What did Tara see when she watched a news story about a volcanic explosion? Complete the sentences with the correct verb in the past continuous.**

film	~~watch~~	do
flow	grow	not live

a While I was watching TV, there was a news story about a volcanic eruption.

b Camera men ____________ the eruption as it happened.

c As the lava ____________ down the mountain, an ash cloud exploded.

d They closed the airport because the ash cloud ____________ bigger.

e Luckily, people ____________ near to the volcano when it erupted.

f What ____________ you ____________ when you saw the volcano?

Practice

2 **Choose the correct form of the verbs to complete the dialogue.**

> **Get it right!**
>
> Remember to use the auxiliary verb, *was* or *were*.
>
> ~~They watching TV~~ ... They **were** watching TV ...

Amir: So, what were you doing when you saw the lightning?

Noah: We [1] **played / were playing** in the park! There were about five of us.

Amir: And what happened next?

Noah: We [2] **had / were having** a game of football when suddenly the sky went dark and there was lightning in the sky. As we were playing, the lightning [3] **struck / was striking** the tree nearby, and as we [4] **looked / were looking** at the tree, a huge branch fell off!

Amir: Scary! [5] **Did anyone stand / Was anyone standing** under the tree?

Noah: No, but Josh [6] **chased / was chasing** the ball near the tree when the lightning [7] **hit / was hitting**.

Amir: Oh no! Did he get hurt?

Noah: No, he [8] **stopped / was stopping** just in time. Then we all started to run away.

Amir: [9] **Did any other branches fall / Were any other branches falling** off?

Noah: I don't know. We didn't wait to see!

3 **Can you sort the words and make questions? Then read the dialogue again and answer the questions.**

a the boys / outside / Were / playing / ? ____________________

b playing / How many / were / boys / ? ____________________

c struck / they / doing / What / were / the lightning / when / ? ____________________

d under / Was / standing / the tree / ? / Josh ____________________

e doing / ? / was / What / he ____________________

Challenge

4 **Have you ever experienced any extreme weather or powerful nature? Write about your experience in your own notebook. Use the past simple and past continuous.**

Last summer I was playing in the ... when I saw ...

7.3 Connecting words

Use of English

Connecting words join two parts of a sentence and show when something happens.

Don't move from where you are **while** the earthquake is happening. (at the same time as)

As soon as the shaking starts, get down on your hands and knees. (immediately after)

Stay inside **until** the shaking stops. (a point in time)

We use *before* and *after* to talk about the order of events in the past or future.

Make sure you know what to do **before** an earthquake happens.

After an earthquake happens, there is usually a lot of damage.

We can put *as soon as*, *before* and *after* at the beginning of a sentence and in the middle. We usually put *while* and *until* in the middle (but sometimes at the beginning too).

You can go outside **as soon as** the storm stops.

While it's raining so hard, you should stay inside.

Focus

1 **What should you do during a strong lightning storm?**
Choose and circle the correct connecting word to complete the advice.

a If you can, move indoors **before / until** the storm starts.

b Stay away from windows **after / while** the winds are very strong.

c Unplug your laptop **as soon as / after** the storm starts.

d Don't use a landline **until / while** the lightning stops.

e You can go outside again **before / after** the storm has finished.

Practice

2 **Read about Anisa's experience of a small earthquake. Choose the correct connecting word to complete her story. You will need to use some of the words more than once.**

> **Get it right!**
>
> Remember to use the correct preposition.
>
> Last month I had a bicycle accident, so my bike was broken ~~**until**~~ **after** that.

until	after	before	as soon as	while

There are always signs [1]______ an earthquake happens; for example, there are power cuts and many animals behave strangely. We knew there was a problem [2]______ the room started shaking. We knew it could be serious, so we hid under a table and stayed there [3]______ the shaking stopped. We were so frightened. We held onto the table legs [4]______ things fell off the shelves and crashed to the floor. We knew an earthquake was happening. We waited, terrified, [5]______ the room stopped moving. It stopped [6]______ a few minutes, but it seemed a lot longer!

[7]______ the shaking stopped, my brother wanted to get up and go outside. But we knew that we should wait a bit [8]______ we moved anywhere. When we were sure that everything was OK, we went outside to see what had happened.

3 **What should you do during an earthquake? Complete the instructions.**

a Make sure you know what to do, **before** the earthquake starts.

b Crawl under a table **as soon as** ______

c Stay inside **while** ______

d Don't move **until** ______

e Stay away from damaged areas **after** ______

Challenge

4 **Choose an example of extreme weather or a natural danger. Answer the questions in your own notebook, using the connecting words.**

a What can you do to prepare **before** it happens?

b What should you do **while** it is happening?

c What should you do **after** it happens?

7.4 The effects of nature's power

1 **Read Rohan's description of his visit to Angkor Wat. Match a photo to each paragraph.**

a

b

c

d

1 Deep in the forests of Cambodia, in south-east Asia, lies the ancient city of Angkor. Beautiful ruined temples cover the huge mysterious site and trees have grown over many of the buildings. Nobody has lived there for over 600 years. But Angkor was once an enormous city, home to 750 000 people. Then suddenly, its people abandoned the city and no one knows why!

2 I visited Angkor last year on holiday with my family. My dad works for a museum and he is really **interested** [1] **on / in** the history of ancient places. He visited Angkor a long time ago, before I was born. He was so **amazed** [2] **by / for** the buildings and the lakes that he wanted his family to see them too.

3 When we visited, we were **surprised** [3] **to / by** how many other tourists were visiting the biggest temples. I felt **sad** [4] **in / about** all the big crowds because I couldn't see anything properly. So, my dad took us to look at the smaller, quieter places instead. And it was amazing! There were places where the jungle was really wild and it looked as if it was eating the temples! We found old rooms too. There were pictures carved from stone on the walls, telling stories of the history and legends of Cambodia.

4 We were **fascinated** [5] **by / for** the mixture of nature and ancient ruins at Angkor. We laughed at the monkeys playing in the ruins. We loved discovering something new and exciting around every corner. I loved imagining what it was like to live in this place hundreds of years ago. But why did the people leave the city so suddenly? I felt sad when I thought about that.

2 **Read the description again and mark the sentences true or false. Can you correct the false sentences?**

a People live in and use the buildings at Angkor now. ____________

b A long time ago, people left the city of Angkor and didn't go back. ____________

c Apart from Rohan's family, there were only a few other visitors to Angkor. ____________

d Rohan and his family only saw the biggest temples. ____________

e Rohan and his sister found the trees and plants growing around the buildings very interesting. ____________

3 **Can you put the headings in the order of Rohan's description?**

a What Rohan saw at Angkor. ______

b Interesting facts about Angkor. ______

c Rohan's feelings about Angkor. ______

d When Rohan visited Angkor and who he was with. ______

4 **Find the adjectives + prepositions in bold in the description. Choose and circle the correct preposition.**

5 **Which information in the text did you think was the most surprising?**

____

____

Writing tip

Include surprising information.

When you describe a place, start with some interesting or surprising information to get the reader's attention.

Challenge

6 **Think of a special place you have visited. Then write a description in four paragraphs in your notebook. Put the paragraphs in the same order as Rohan's description.**

7.5 Thank You Letter

1 **Read the poem *Thank You Letter* by Eric Finney again. Choose and circle the correct answer to complete the sentences about the poem.**

a The writer thanks the sun for the times it **rises / rises and goes down**.

b He says that the sun is **sometimes late / always on time**.

c He says that the sun **makes grey days brighter / is always behind a cloud**.

d He thanks the sun for **shining on everyone's face / making the whole world feel happy**.

e He thanks the sun for **burning beaches / making beaches hot and bright**.

f He thanks the sun for **producing fruit / making fruit ready to eat**.

g He thanks the sun for sharing its **heat / light**.

h He says to the sun, 'We know how **valuable / hot** you are.'

2 Vocabulary: **Replace the underlined words with a word from the box.**

sunset	~~blazing~~	ripening	glow	at dawn

a The sun is <u>hot and bright</u> today. Don't go outside without a sun hat! blazing

b We got up <u>very early in the morning</u> to watch the sun rise. The air felt very warm and fresh. ______

c The <u>shining light</u> of the sun can be very powerful – take your sunglasses! ______

d It is early evening now and the <u>sun going down</u> is really beautiful – a fireball of orange, red and purple. ______

e The fruit on the tree is <u>becoming ready to eat</u>. Tomorrow we'll pick it and prepare it for dinner. ______

3 **Say the words from the poem to yourself.**
Which consonant and vowel sounds are the same in each group?
Underline the letters that make the sounds.

a glow / know b grace / face c say / day d great / late

4 Write: **Can you complete the poem with the words in the box?**
Look at the words in bold to help you find rhyming words and matching sounds.

night	shapes	magical	awake

Dear magnificent moon
Just a line to **say**,
Thanks for your changing [1]__________,
And luminous white **light**.
You hide all **day**,
And shine bright at [2]__________.
You keep me [3]__________
And make me **play**.
Mysterious [4]__________ moon.

Challenge

5 Values: **Use the guide to write your own short poem about something you are thankful for. Here are some ideas to help you. Use words that have a similar or matching sound, if you can (it doesn't have to rhyme).**

Dear ...
Just a line to say,
Thanks for (adjective / noun)
And (adjective / noun)
You (verb phrase)...
And (verb phrase)...
(adjective / adjective / noun)

a natural wonder
a special place
a special person
a special animal

7.6 Check your progress

Choose the correct answers and write in the space.

1 The volcano ____________ while we were making the video.

a erupting b erupted c erupts

2 We ____________ driving in the car when we saw the lightning.

a was b wasn't c were

3 When the top of the volcano ____________, it threw hundreds of rocks into the air.

a exploded b pushed c hit

4 The earthquake made ____________ in the side of the house, but it didn't fall down.

a craters b flows c cracks

5 In a storm cloud, pieces of ice ____________ into each other.

a connect b bump c erupt

6 Lightning can ____________ tall objects such as trees and towers.

a bump b rise c strike

7 If there is an earthquake, you should ____________ under a table.

a run b crawl c walk

8 To protect yourself, you should ____________ your head with your arm.

a hold on b cover c touch

9 We didn't move ____________ the room stopped shaking.

a while b as soon as c until

10 At sunset, on a clear evening, the sun ____________ red and orange.

a lights b shows c glows

7.7 Reflection

Think about what you have studied in this unit. Answer the questions.

1 What topics did you like and why?

____

____

2 What activities did you like and why?

____

____

3 What did you find challenging and why?

____

____

4 What help do you need now?

____

____

5 What do you want to find out more about?

____

____

8 Entertainment

8.1 Entertainment at home

1 **Look at the word puzzle. Can you find six words to match the definitions?**

a The music for a film or TV programme. ____________

b The clothes actors wear to look like someone else. ____________

c All the actors who play characters in a film. ____________

d A way of making moving images with still pictures. ____________

e The special effects that you hear on screen. ____________

f Images and designs that you see on screen. ____________

2 **Sort the words in Activity 1 and write in the categories. Which words belong to more than one category?**

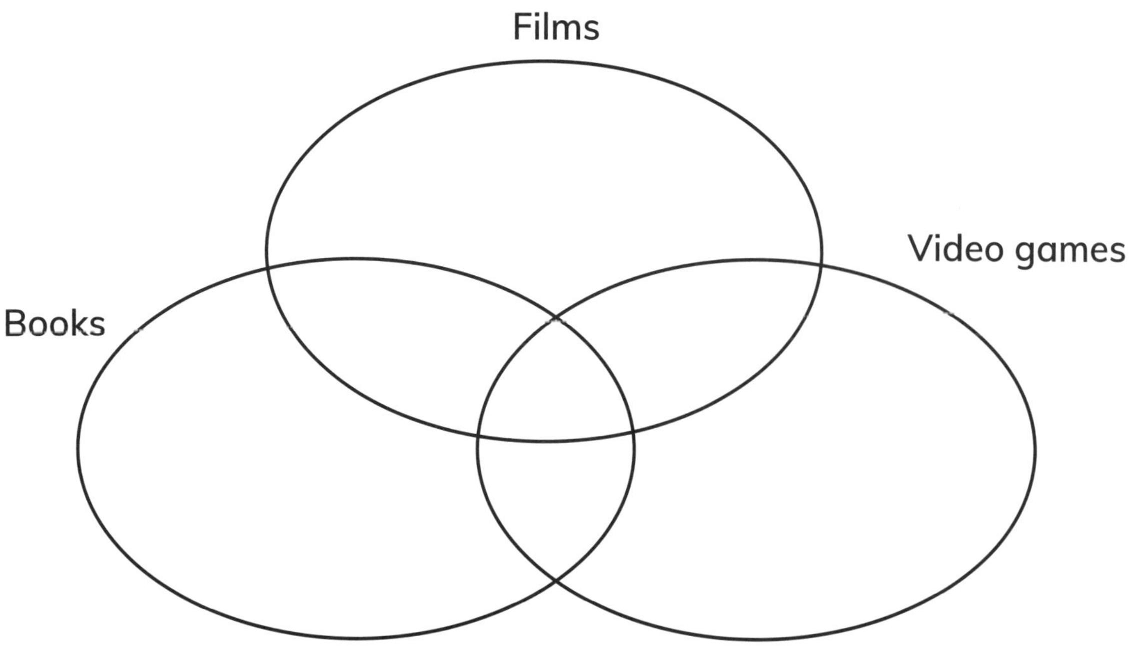

3 **Read Jian's comments about the film Jungle Book. Match questions a–d to Jian's answers.**

a Why did you like it so much?

b What's it about?

c Have you seen any good films recently?

d What kind of film is it?

1 Yes, I have. Last weekend I watched the film Jungle Book with my friends. Have you seen it? It's awesome! ________

2 It's an adventure film. It's exciting, frightening, funny and sad all at the same time. ________

3 It's about a young boy called Mowgli who grows up in the jungle with a family of wolves. But one day a huge tiger threatens to kill him, so other animals help him escape. But Mowgli doesn't want to leave, because the jungle is his home ... ________

4 I loved it because the plot is really exciting and the special effects are amazing. There is a young actor who plays Mowgli, but all the animal characters are made with animation and they look so real! One of my friends was really frightened by the snake in the film. I was scared of the tiger! The animal characters all speak and their voices all come from famous actors. The jungle setting looks so real too. It made me interested in real jungles.

4 **Read Jian's comments again and answer the questions.**

a Which paragraph tells you about the **plot**? ________________

b Where is the **setting** for the film? ________________

c Who is the main **character**? ________________

d What is special about the other **characters**? ________________________________

5 **Find and <u>underline</u> examples of participle adjectives in Jian's comments in Activity 3.**

Challenge

6 **In your notebook, write about a film that you have seen. Answer the questions a–d in Activity 3.**

8.2 Past simple passive

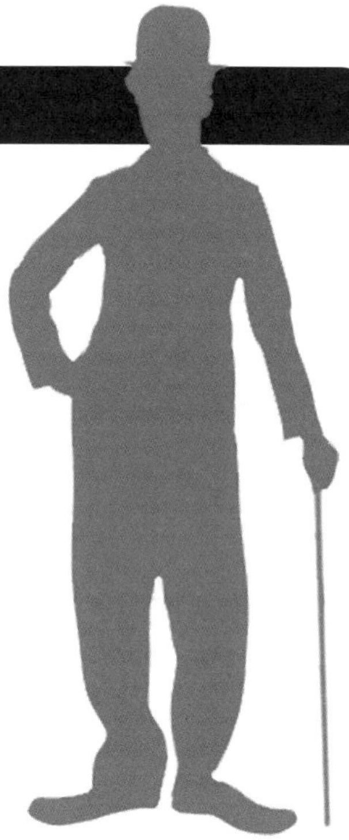

Use of English

We use this passive form to talk about past events. We use it when we want to focus on the event, not the person who did it (or when we don't know who did it).

We make the **past simple passive** with the past form of the verb be (*was* / *were*) + past participle.

These early films ***were made*** *in black and white.*

If we want to mention the person who did the action, we use *by*.

In 1891, the first film projector ***was invented by*** *the Edison company.*

We make the negative form with *wasn't* / *weren't* (*was* / *were not*) + past participle.

Sound ***wasn't added*** *to films until the 1920s.*

We use question word + was / were + past participle to make questions.

What was *the first animated film* ***called****?*

We use was / were + past participle to make yes / no questions.

Was *the first cinema* ***opened*** *in 1905? Yes, it* ***was****.*

Focus

1 **Complete the facts about film animation using the past simple passive.**

a Lots of Disney films <u>were produced</u> (produce) in the 1960s and 70s.

b The first cartoons ______________ (draw) by hand.

c In the first cartoons, hundreds of drawings ______________ (need) to produce just one minute of animation.

d The first animated film ______________ (not make) in colour.

e Computers ______________ (not use) to create these early cartoons.

f The first *Toy Story* film ______________ (create) in the 1990s.

g The animated film *Shrek* ______________ (release) in 2001.

Practice

2 **Read about the history of animation. Look at the verbs in 1–7. Can you correct the errors? Write the corrections at the end.**

> **Get it right!**
>
> Remember to use the auxiliary verb, *was* or *were* and the correct past participle.
>
> The first films ~~made~~ **were made** in black and white.

A brief history of animation

1900s: The first animated films [1]were make were made from drawings. The drawings [2]were do ______________ by hand and took a long time.

1928: Sound was added to cartoons for the first time. Mickey Mouse was also born!

1937: *Snow White and the Seven Dwarves*, the first full-length animated film, [3]were produced ______________ by Walt Disney, the owner of Disney.

1940s–1950s: Disney films became popular and [4]were watch ______________ by millions of people in cinemas.

1990s: Computers [5]was used ______________ for the first time to make animated films.

1995: *Toy Story* [6]was release ______________ – the first full-length film that was animated on computers.

2002: *Shrek*, one of the most popular animated films of all time, became the first animated film to win an Oscar (a very big film award). It had a clever storyline and [7]were made ______________ with fantastic computer-generated special effects.

Challenge

3 **Which animated films do you like? Write a short paragraph about your favourite animated film. Add an image from the film in the box.**

______________ was released in ______________.

The main character is ______________

____

____

____

8.3 Adverbs of time and frequency

Use of English

These **adverbs** describe when an action happens.
Some adverbs can describe definite (exact) time:

We've talked **today** about what you do on your devices.

Definite adverbs such as ***yesterday, today, tonight*** and ***tomorrow*** often go at the beginning or end of the sentence.

Tomorrow you can play video games, but not now.
We didn't have any screen time **yesterday**.

Definite adverbs such as ***hourly, daily, weekly*** (that measure time) go at the end of a sentence.

How much time do you spend on your tablet **weekly**?

Some adverbs don't specify an exact time (indefinite adverbs):

I **often** use my tablet for schoolwork.

Indefinite adverbs usually go **after** the pronoun and **before** the main verb in a sentence or question. BUT the adverb goes **after** the pronoun **and** the verb *to be*.

We **sometimes use** a Maths website to help with our homework.
He **is always** on his phone!

Focus

1 **Sort the words to make sentences about screen time in Nina's family.**

a about ten hours of screen time / I / weekly / have / .

b daily / doesn't / My family / watch TV / .

c about an hour online every day / I / spend / usually / .

d often / I / online / am / for more than an hour at the weekends / .

e video calls to our friends / make / My family / occasionally / .

f to do my homework / I am using / today / my tablet / .

2 **How similar are Nina's screen habits to yours?**
Tick (✓) the sentences in Activity 1 that are true for you.

Practice

3 **Aran is telling his mum about his class's screen time survey. Complete the conversation by writing in the correct option (a or b) for 1–6.**

> **Get it right!**
>
> Remember to put the adverb in the correct position in the sentence.
>
> We ~~go always~~ **always go** online in the evening.

Mum: So what did you do at school [1]______________?

Aran: Our class did a survey about screen time. We asked each other how much time we all spend on our devices.

Mum: Mmm interesting! Were you at the top? You are [2]______________ on your tablet! I've asked you to keep your screen time to one hour a day. At least during the school term …

Aran: I do try, Mum! But I [3]____________ use my tablet to do my homework. [4]______________ I looked at a science website.

Mum: Yes, that's ok. But you don't only use it for homework, do you?

Aran: No, I know I use it a lot but some of my friends are worse. Sam [5]______________ spends three hours a day online. But we made a class promise to reduce our screen time. And we are going to review it [6]______________.

Mum: What a great idea! Let's see if habits change in a few weeks' time …

1	a usually	b today	2	a always	b hourly
3	a daily	b usually	4	a Yesterday	b Sometimes
5	a daily	b sometimes	6	a always	b monthly

Challenge

4 **Write sentences about your screen habits in your notebook. Use the adverbs in the box to help you.**

always	normally	usually	sometimes	occasionally
daily	weekly	today	tonight	tomorrow

I normally spend more time online at the weekends.

8.4 Creating film scenes

1 **Read the storyboard text (1–4) and put the pictures in the correct order. What kind of film do you think it is?** ______________

The Light in the Garden

1 It was already past midnight and Lily couldn't sleep. She didn't know why. Then she realised that her sister Lara was awake too …

2 Lily got up to close the curtain. It seemed unusually bright outside for a cloudy winter night. Then she noticed the light in the corner of the garden.

3 Lara got out of bed and joined Lily at the window. The two girls looked at the light in amazement. Lara wanted to go outside and look at it close up.

4 Lily looked at her sister in shock. She didn't want to go out in the cold dark garden in the middle of the night. But her sister had other ideas!

a ______

b ______

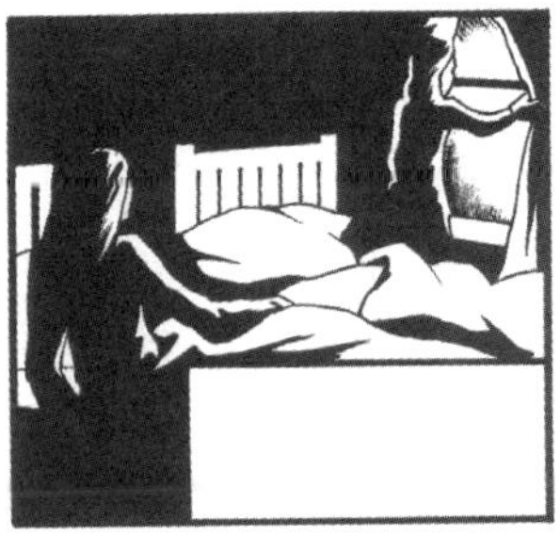

c ______

d ___1___

2 **Punctuation: Direct speech**

Add speech marks, exclamation marks and commas to the dialogue. Use the example to help you.

1 'You are joking!' exclaimed Lily, 'I'm not going out there at this time of night!'

'Well, I'll go on my own then,' replied Lara. 'I want to find out what it is.'

2 Hey, Lara Are you awake too? I can't sleep whispered Lily.

Me neither. I've been awake for hours replied Lara.

3 It's some kind of light. But where's it coming from? wondered Lara.

Let's go and have a look.

4 Lara, come and have a look at this What do you think it is?

3 **Match the dialogue in Activity 3 with the pictures from Activity 2.**

1b

4 Vocabulary: **Reporting verbs**

Complete each sentence below with a verb from the word box.

sniggered	whispered	~~sighed~~	asked	insisted

a 'Oh no! You've done it again! I'm tired of it! Don't you ever learn?' Dad sighed.

b 'You must come with us! I won't take no for an answer!' he ______.

c 'It's so funny! He still doesn't realise that he's put his tent on the ants' nest!' he ______.

d 'What time is it?' she ______ for the third time.

e 'Shh! Don't speak so loudly! They'll hear you!' she ______.

Challenge

5 **What do you think happens in the next two scenes of *The Light in the Garden*? Write sentences and dialogues in your notebook.**

8.5 *Jurassic Park*

1 **Complete the summary of the *Jurassic Park* film story with words from the box.**

controlled	science-fiction	dinosaurs	island
escape	breaks	scientists	

Jurassic Park is a [1] science-fiction film. It is about a group of [2]__________ who visit an [3]__________ inhabited by [4]__________. Before the scientists arrive, the dinosaurs live in a [5]__________ area on the island and they can't escape. But then someone [6]__________ the security code and the dinosaurs escape. The scientists and other people on the island try to [7]__________ from the dinosaurs.

2 **Why is *Jurassic Park* famous in cinema history? Circle the correct answer.**

a It starred lots of famous actors.

b It showed computer-generated special effects that were new at the time.

c It is one of the most terrifying films ever made.

3 **Read the extract again from the novel *Jurassic Park* by Michael Crichton. Put the pictures from the story in the correct order.**

a  ☐

b  ☐

c  ☐

d  ☐

e  1

f  ☐

4 **Choose and underline the correct answer.**

1 Tina and her parents are at the beach. Her parents are a) **next to her.** b) quite far from her.

2 Tina wants to be a) **on her own.** b) **with her parents.**

3 Tina a) **stays by the sea.** b) **moves under the palm trees.**

4 In the sand, she notices a) **birds.** b) **bird footprints.**

5 Next, she sees a lizard a) **coming towards her.** b) **running away into the bushes.**

6 The lizard is a) **afraid.** b) **not afraid of Tina.**

7 Tina thinks that the lizard a) **wants to play.** b) **wants some food.**

8 The lizard jumps onto Tina's a) **hand.** b) **toes.**

9 The lizard is a) **heavy.** b) **not heavy.**

5 **How do you work out unknown words in a sentence when you are reading? Tick (✓) the strategy that will help you guess meaning from context.**

a Don't read the sentence. Read only the word and try and guess it. ☐

b Read the whole sentence to get an idea of the word's meaning. ☐

c Check the dictionary first. ☐

6 Word study: **Read the sentences from the story. Underline the words that help you understand the meaning of the words in bold.**

a Tina decided to move out of the sun, back from the water, to the **shade** of the palm trees.

b The lizard stood on its **hind** legs, balancing on its thick tail ...

c ... the lizard jumped onto her hand. Tina could feel its little toes pinching the skin of her **palm** and she felt the surprising **weight** of the animal's body pressing her arm down.

d And then the lizard **scrambled** up her arm, toward her face.

8.6 Check your progress

1 **Can you complete the descriptions of film types with words from the box?**

comedy	~~adventure~~	horror	drama	science-fiction	action

a Adventure films are sometimes set in a fantasy place. The story is often about how the main character overcomes a problem or dilemma.

b ______________ films are supposed to make you feel really scared.

c ______________ films are set in the future. They're often set in space.

d In ______________ films, there is usually a hero in a dangerous, exciting situation. These films are fast-moving and usually very noisy.

e ______________ films make you laugh a lot and are not very serious.

f ______________ films are usually about serious situations in life.

2 **In your notebook, make questions in the past simple passive with the words below.**

a Who / Snow White and the Seven Dwarves / produce / by?
Who was Snow White and the Seven Dwarves produced by?

b What / use / to make animation films from the 1990s?

c How / cartoons / draw / in the 1900s?

d When / sound / add / to cartoons?

e When / the animation film, *Shrek*, / release?

f When / the first *Toy Story* film / make?

3 **Write the answers to the questions in Activity 2. Find the answers on page 95.**

a ______________ b ______________ c ______________

d ______________ e ______________ f ______________

Challenge

4 **Choose a character from your favourite film, book, TV programme or video game. Write three questions to ask that character. Imagine and write their answers.**

8.7 Reflection

Think about what you have studied in this unit. Answer the questions.

1 What topics did you like and why?

____

____

2 What activities did you like and why?

____

____

3 What did you find challenging and why?

____

____

4 What help do you need now?

____

____

5 What do you want to find out more about?

____

____

9 Amazing art

9.1 Amazing art around us

1 Vocabulary: **Match the words to the definitions.**

sculpture	3D	metal	textiles	mural	pattern
doorway	steel	spray paint	mosaic	paper	concrete

a Pieces of fabric that are made by hand or a machine. __________

b A large picture painted on a wall. __________

c A design with repeated shapes, lines or colours. __________

d A strong metal that can be shiny or dull. __________

e This adjective means 'three dimensional'. It is the opposite of 'flat'. __________

f A pattern or picture made with lots of small pieces of coloured glass or stone. __________

2 **Use the words in Activity 1 to answer the questions.**

a Use three words from Activity 1 to describe the artwork in the photos. Which do you prefer? Why?

b Find five words for materials that can be used to create artworks.

c Find a word to describe the area around a door.

d Look around you. Which objects are decorated with a pattern?

3 **Sasha and her uncle are talking about art. Complete the conversation with the correct indefinite pronouns.**

everyone	somewhere	~~everywhere~~
nobody	something	anything

Uncle: So, are there many places to see art where you live?
Sasha: Not really. But when I think about it, art is [1] ___everywhere___ in my school.
Uncle: That's interesting. Where can you see art in your school?
Sasha: Well, first there's the mural on the playground wall – Year 4 students painted that last year. It shows flags from all the different nationalities of students we have in our school.
Uncle: What a great idea! Anything else?
Sasha: Yes, there's a big 3D model of the school in the entrance hall. It was in our headteacher's office, but [2] ____________ could see it there. So, she moved it to a place where everybody could see it. And there is always [3] ____________ on the wall in our classroom from our art class. At the moment, [4] ____________ has their work on display – that's thirty pieces of art!
Uncle: Is there [5] ____________ else you would like to see on display at school?
Sasha: Yes, I'd like to see another mural – I think they are fun!
Uncle: Is there [6] ____________ where students could paint another mural?
Sasha: Yes, I think so. There is an empty wall by the sports hall – we could paint one there!

4 **Read the conversation again and answer the questions.**

a Is there **anywhere** in Sasha's school where you can see art? Where? What can you see?

b Is there **anything** on the wall in Sasha's classroom? What?

c Why couldn't **anyone** see the 3D model at first?

d Is there **anything** that Sasha would like to see in her school now? What?

Challenge

5 **You are going to design a piece of art for a school. Choose one of the options below. Make notes and design it in your notebook.**

1 Design another mural for Sasha's school. What is the subject of the mural in her playground? What might be suitable for the wall near the sports hall?

2 Design a piece of art for your school. What kind of art will it be? What subject might be suitable? Where can people see it?

9.2 Present perfect for unfinished past

Use of English

The **present perfect** can be used to talk about the **unfinished past**. It connects a past situation to the present in some way.

I'**ve had** two music classes **this week**. ('this week' hasn't finished yet)

It is also used to talk about an indefinite time in the past.

I'**ve made** my sculpture out of recycled objects. (recent 'indefinite' past)

In contrast we use the past simple to talk about a finished action in a definite time.

Yesterday, I **made** a wind instrument called a kazoo.

↑

Definite time

Focus

1 **Read the text about recycled art.**
Use the verbs in the box to complete the text.
Use the present perfect.

use	not have	~~become~~
visit	throw away	

There is a saying that, 'One person's trash is another's treasure'. Recycled art [1] has become very popular over the past decade. Artists who specialise in this form of art use all kinds of materials people [2] ____________, such as: plastic bottles, car tyres, cans and plastic toys.

Here the artist [3] ____________ old car tyres, buckets, spades and watering cans to make a gigantic fish. Thousands of people [4] ____________ it since it went on display in March. If you [5] ____________ the chance to see it yet, it's well worth a visit!

Get it right!

Remember to use the present perfect for the 'unfinished past'. Don't use the past simple.

~~I had two exams so far today.~~ **I've had** two exams **so far today**.

Practice

2 **Max and Mia are talking about a music project. Complete the dialogue using the past simple or present perfect of the verb in brackets.**

Max: 1 Have you made **(make)** the instrument for the music project yet?

Mia: No, I haven't, I 2 ______ **(do)** some research online yesterday though. I 3 ______ **(decide)** to make a rain stick. It's a percussion instrument and it looks quite easy to make. Yesterday, I 4 ______ **(find)** a long, cardboard tube and an old balloon I can use, too. 5 ______ you ______ **(finish)** your instrument yet?

Max: No, not yet. I 6 ______ **(not have)** time, but I 7 ______ **(draw)** a design for it last weekend. It's called a Kazoo. It's easy to play and makes a cool, buzzing sound when you blow into it.

Mia: It'll be fun to hear all the instruments the class 8 ______ **(make)** in music class on Wednesday. I can't wait!

Challenge

3 **Complete these sentences about what you have done/haven't done at school today. Use the present perfect.**

a I've chatted to my friends during break time.

b ______ yet.

c ______ already.

d ______ this morning.

9.3 Present tenses with future meaning

Use of English

Present tenses with future meaning

We use the present simple for events in the future which are certain because they are facts, or because there is a fixed schedule.

SEPTEMBER

Sun	Mon	Tues	Wed	Thurs	Fri	Sat
30	31	1	2	3	4 School starts	5
6	7	8	9	10	11	12
13	14	15	16	17	18	19

Their train **leaves** early on Wednesday morning ...
The new school term **doesn't start** until September.
What time **does** the museum **close** in the summer?

We can use the present continuous to talk about the future. It shows that we have already decided something and that we have already made a plan or arrangements.

They **are arriving** on Sunday and **staying** until Wednesday.
Dom **is meeting** his cousin next week for a day out.
They **aren't visiting** the sculpture park at the weekend anymore. They've changed their plans.
What **are** you **doing** on Thursday? I'**m going** to see the Star Circus.

Focus

1 **Lila and Erin are messaging each other to plan a day out. Choose and circle the correct tense to complete their messages.**

What time [1] **do we meet / are we meeting** on Tuesday? [2] **Do you get / Are you getting** the bus into town?

Yes, but I'm not sure what time. The bus timetable [3] **changes / is changing** during the summer. I'll find out!

I think the buses [4] **leave / are leaving** every half an hour from next week. Let me know! And what about lunch?

[5] **We eat / We're eating** at the pizza restaurant. My mum's already booked it for 1pm.

Are you sure it's the pizza restaurant?

Yes, I'm sure because they [6] **have got / are getting** a meal deal at lunchtimes all next week!

Practice

2 **Mr Cheng is checking arrangements for his class's art workshop. Complete the email with the correct form of the present simple or present continuous and the verbs in the box.**

> **Get it right!**
>
> Remember to use the present continuous for plans that are already arranged.
>
> Next week my cousins ~~will come~~ **are coming** to my house.
> I ~~will go~~ **am going** to a theatre show next weekend.

open	bring	~~start~~	meet	spend	not have	leave	arrive

New Message

To: Cc Bcc

Subject:

Dear Class 6A

As you know, our summer art programme 1 starts on Monday 25 July at River Park, which is a short train ride away from the city centre. I have already sent your parents and carers the arrangements for the day, so here is a reminder for you.

We 2 ____________ at 9 a.m. at City Street train station. The train 3 ____________ at 9.30 a.m., so please don't be late. When we get to the park, there will be time for snacks, because we 4 ____________ lunch until 2 p.m. This is so we can spend time taking photos in the new Sculpture Garden. This new garden only 5 ____________ from 9–2 p.m. in the summer months, so we want to make the most of it!

And we have a special surprise for you! Ms Sol, your art teacher from last year, 6 ____________ this week from her new home in the USA. She 7 ____________ the day with us and we've invited her to give you a multimedia workshop in the afternoon. She 8 ____________ all her best ideas to give you a really fun tutorial, using natural materials in the park. She can't wait to see you all again!

See you all on Monday!

Mr Cheng

Send

Challenge

3 **Imagine you are going on a trip to a special place or event. Write an email to a friend telling him or her about the plans.**

- Where are you going?
- What time does it start? What are the travel arrangements?
- What are the other plans for the day or evening?

9.4 Amazing architecture

1 **Match the descriptive words to the buildings.**

curved ☐	colourful pipes ☐	wavy ☐
gleaming ☐	smooth ☐	metallic ☐

A

Pompidou Centre, Paris, France

B

Heydar-aliyer centre, Baku, Azerbaijan

2 **Read the poem about one of the buildings from Activity 1. Which building is being described?**

1 I look like a ship in a port,
2 I am made of steel pipes and gleaming glass.
3 I'm futuristic, strange and wonderful,
4 I tower over the city streets.
5 I am filled with art and music.
6 What am I?

☐

3 **Match the questions to a line in the poem.**

a What are you like? Line 3

b What's inside you? ______

c What is around you? ______

d What do you look like? ______

e What are you made of? ______

4 **Which building do you like best? Explain why.**

I like ______________________

____

____

5 **What do buildings A and B *look like* to you? Write a sentence about each one.**

____

____

____

Writing tip

Plan your work

Take time to think about what you are going to write before you start writing.

6 **Write a poem about amazing architecture in your country or town. First make notes about it using these prompts to help you.**

- I look like ______________________
- I'm made of ______________________
- I'm (shape, material, colour) ______________________
- Inside ______________________
- Around me ______________________

7 **Now write your poem in your notebook. Use your notes and the poem in Activity 2 to help you.**

9.5 Willow

1 **Read the story of *Willow* in the Learner's Book again and circle if the sentences are true (T) or false (F). Correct the false sentences in your notebook.**

a Miss Hawthorn's art room was a bright sunny place. **True / False**

b All the students painted the trees in different styles. **True / False**

c Willow painted a different coloured tree. **True / False**

d Miss Hawthorn thinks that Willow's tree painting is very unusual. **True / False**

e Miss Hawthorn liked Willow because she showed her pictures from her art book.**True / False**

f Miss Hawthorn liked the way that Willow painted the objects in her art class. **True / False**

g No one bought a present for Miss Hawthorn apart from Willow. **True / False**

h At the end of the story, Miss Hawthorn started to experiment with a different style of drawing. **True / False**

2 Vocabulary: **Complete the sentences with a word from the box.**

glared	giggled	frown	shivered	scowl

a We ____________ with fright as we entered the cold dark house.

b You could see that he was confused by the ____________ on his face.

c 'I don't want to go swimming. I hate it!' said my sister with a ____________.

d We all ____________ when Dad kept calling my friend by the wrong name.

e During the movie, people ____________ at my mum when she answered her phone for the third time.

3 **Read the table and check the adjective order in phrases 1–8 below. Which phrases are correct and incorrect? Correct the incorrect phrases.**

Use of English

Adjective order

We use more than one adjective before a noun, to describe something in more detail.

There wasn't a **single broken** crayon in the bunch.

Number / quantity	Opinion	Size	Physical quality (e.g. texture, taste)	Colour	Material (or type)	Noun
single			broken			crayon
			soft		furry	kitten

1 a delicious hot chicken dinner ______ ☐

2 brown creamy chocolate ice cream ______ ☐

3 an exciting noisy football match ______ ☐

4 a blue quiet beautiful lake ______ ☐

5 a colourful big circus show ______ ☐

6 an white enormous bright flash of lightning ______ ☐

7 a yellow soft cute baby chick ______ ☐

8 a huge metal shiny sculpture ______ ☐

4 **Read the list in Activity 3 again. Put a tick (✓) next to the phrases that describe things that you have seen or experienced.**

5 Values: **Thinking in a creative way**

Think about other things that ***stimulate your senses.***
Write phrases to describe these things using two or more adjectives.

a Your favourite food ______

b Something you like to look at ______

c A favourite place ______

d A favourite animal ______

e A type of weather you have experienced ______

9.6 Check your progress

1 **Complete the crossword. Read the clues to find the missing words.**

Across →

1 The ability to produce or use new ideas.
8 The ability to focus and pay attention to something you are doing.
10 A hard grey material that is used for building.
11 An adjective that means 'rounded shape'.

Down ↓

2 The ability to create pictures in your mind or have new ideas.
3 Cloth that is often woven or knitted.
4 You can see flags made of this material in Mexico at festival time.
5 A sculpture of a well-known person.
6 A game or competition where you answer questions.
7 A meeting for people to learn how to do or make something.
9 A place where you can see plays and performances on a stage.

Challenge

2 **Make a revision crossword to test your friends.**

9.7 Reflection

Think about what you have studied in this unit. Answer the questions.

1 What topics did you like and why?

____

____

2 What activities did you like and why?

____

____

3 What did you find challenging and why?

____

____

4 What help do you need now?

____

____

5 What do you want to find out more about?

____

____

Acknowledgements

The authors and publishers acknowledge the following sources of copyright material and are grateful for the permissions granted. While every effort has been made, it has not always been possible to identify the sources of all the material used, or to trace all copyright holders. If any omissions are brought to our notice, we will be happy to include the appropriate acknowledgements on reprinting.

Illustration by Tony Ross from *Billionaire Boy* by David Walliams © 2010 Reprinted by permission of HarperCollins Publishers Ltd

Illustrations from *Willow* by Denise Brennan-Nelson and Rosemarie Brennan. Used with the permission of Sleeping Bear Press.

Thanks to the following for permission to reproduce images:

Cover by Omar Aranda (Beehive Illustraion); *Inside* **Unit 1**: Jose Luis Pelaez Inc/GI; Ian. CuiYi/GI; Oliver Strewe/GI; Travelpix Ltd/GI; PeopleImages/GI; Valeriy_G/GI; BJI/Blue Jean Images/GI; **Unit 2**: Camille Tokerud/GI; Noah Clayton/GI; Katelyn Mulcahy/GI; Max Mumby/Indigo/GI; **Unit 3**: Martin Ruegner/GI; Francois Gohier/GI; Reptiles4all/GI; Travelpix Ltd/GI; James Hipps/GI; Mehmet zhan Araboga/GI; Kuritafsheen/GI; Kuritafsheen/GI; Peter Adams/GI; Malven57/GI; Sandra standbridge/GI; Kuritafsheen/GI; Siegfried Layda/GI; Klaus-Werner Friedrich/GI; George Karbus/GI; Damocean/GI; Rebecca R Jackrel/GI; CR Courson/GI; **Unit 4**: Kenneth-cheung/GI; Clu/GI; Filo/GI; Phwphr bdinthr phathr/GI; Jupiterimages/GI; Coddy/GI; Suriyo Hmun Kaew/GI; Jose A. Bernat Bacete/GI; Filipovic018/GI; miflippo/GI; JupiterImages/GI; **Unit 5**: Clubfoto/GI; NoDerog/GI; Richard Sharrocks/GI; Fuse/GI; Francesco Carta fotografo/GI; **Unit 6**: Yulia Naumenko/GI; CTRPhotos/GI; Colin Anderson Productions pty ltd/GI; NASA/Bryan Allen/GI; **Unit 7**: Stocktrek/GI; Sharply_done/GI; Kriangkrai Thitimakorn/GI; Sharon Lapkin/GI; Deborah Pollitt/GI; Richard Sharrocks/GI; Boy_Anupong/GI; Joseph Johnson/GI; Allan Davey/GI; Tom Pfeiffer/VolcanoDiscovery/GI; **Unit 8**: AF archive/Alamy Stock Photo; BaloOm Studios/GI; Jaguar PS/Shutterstock; Cjp/GI; PhotoAlto/Dominique Bruneton/GI; Science Photo Library - Leonello Calvetti/GI **Unit 9**: Stephen Simpson Inc/GI; Image Source/GI; Apisit Sakornkajorndej/GI; James D.Morgan/GI; Truvi/GI; Andrea Pistolesi/GI; digitalimagination/GI; Mladen Antonov/GI; Atlantide Phototravel/GI; Russell Monk/GI; Zetter/GI

Key: GI= Getty Images